Gifts of the Spirit

Gifts
of the Spirit

Kenneth Cain Kinghorn

Abingdon Press

Nashville　　　　　　　　　　　　New York

GIFTS OF THE SPIRIT

Copyright © 1976 by Abingdon Press

Library of Congress Cataloging in Publication Data
Kinghorn, Kenneth C
  Gifts of the spirit.
  Includes index.
  1. Gifts, Spiritual. I. Title.
BT767.3.K56   234'.1   75-22268

ISBN 0-687-14695-X

Scripture quotations unless otherwise noted are from the
Revised Standard Version of the Bible, copyrighted 1946,
1952, and 1971 by the Division of Christian Education,
National Council of Churches, and are used by permission.

Scripture quotations noted NEB are from the New English
Bible. © the Delegates of the Oxford University Press and the
Syndics of the Cambridge University Press 1961, 1970.
Reprinted by permission.

Scripture quotations noted Phillips are from The New
Testament in Modern English, copyright 1958 by J. B. Phillips.

MANUFACTURED BY THE PARTHENON PRESS AT
NASHVILLE, TENNESSEE, UNITED STATES OF AMERICA

Preface

The growing interest in the gifts of the Holy Spirit is one of the significant religious developments of our era. Opinions on spiritual gifts vary to a remarkable degree. Unfortunately, in some cases, the diverse viewpoints have spawned confusion among sincere Christians. On the positive side though, this developing interest in spiritual gifts has contributed to spiritual renewal and stimulated helpful biblical research in this important area of the Christian life.

Throughout my research for this book, I've sought to allow the biblical evidence to guide my conclusions. I've also tried to listen to those who represent the several streams of Christian theology. Most certainly, I have not attempted to wage verbal war with any who might see things differently than I do.

This volume, as is the case with my other books, was written for the non-specialist. The professional scholars can fend for themselves. To my way of thinking, ordinary Christians possess more spiritual perception than scholars usually give them credit for having; but they enjoy less time for study than is sometimes assumed. I've found that persons want meat, not milk. But they want their meat cut up in reasonably manageable pieces. And one other thing—they like the fat trimmed off where possible.

I have a settled conviction that we should approach Christian subjects with mind and heart. Christ calls us to an *understanding* of his truth. But his truth is infinite, and we aren't. So when our intellects come up short, we must approach some theological matters *devotionally*. In this book I have sought to instruct and to inspire, to sharpen understanding and to stimulate commitment.

I've written with a desire to help quell division among Christians, whether actual or potential. I also reverently hope that those who read about the gifts of the Spirit will personally experience the reality of this neglected dimension of Christian experience.

Kenneth Cain Kinghorn

Contents

Chapter I

Where We've Been and Where We Are

Throughout the church Christians have developed an unprecedented interest in the gifts of the Holy Spirit. In many places discussion centers upon such topics as prophecy, healing, tongues, and faith. The Christian community, traditionally concerned with spiritual *fruits,* has now expanded its attention to include spiritual *gifts.* The rediscovery of this New Testament theme constitutes a breakthrough for the church that may prove to be one of the most significant religious developments of our century.

Whenever Christians rediscover a neglected feature of the biblical message, they often tend, in their zeal, to overemphasize their new awareness. For this reason, it is wise for thinking Christians to keep both a biblical and a historical perspective in order to maintain balance.

Let's look, therefore, at some of the background factors leading up to the current explosion of interest in spiritual gifts.

After the apostolic era, problems of heresy and schism challenged the post–New Testament church. The church responded to these threats by developing its creeds, its canon of scripture, and its clergy. As it struggled for institutional stability, the early church neglected to teach very much about the inner work of the Holy Spirit. Consequently, the gifts of the Holy Spirit received little attention. As the Christian community worked out its doctrine and structure, it lost some of the vitality that had characterized the church in the book of Acts.

During the second century certain prophets, called pneumatics, attempted to correct the sagging spiritual life of the church. These persons spearheaded a renewal movement which promised new life for Christians. In spite of the fact that many of these prophets preached the good news of Christ, their movement produced serious problems for the church. Although most of these revivalists appear to have had a vital experience of God, they often made unreasonable claims as to their own authority. Some of them insisted, "After us there will be no further word from God."

Montanus, one of these second-century pneumatics, represents their attempt to bring spiritual renewal to the church. His ministry crystallized into a schismatic movement, called

Montanism. This movement reacted against growing secular tendencies within the church. Montanists emphasized the immediate working of the Holy Spirit, apart from sermon or sacrament. Montanism insisted on a thoroughgoing separation from "the world," in preparation for the expected immediate return of Christ. The Montanists, although pure in intention, erred in insisting on an excessive supernaturalism and a radical puritanism.

Because of Montanism's dogmatism, emotionalism, and divisive ways, the church rejected the movement and spurned its efforts to bring about spiritual renewal. Any good that Montanism might have done was mostly cancelled by its fanatical fervor and its unorthodox methods. Rather than renew the church, Montanism only divided it.

In rejecting Montanism, the church overreacted. Christian leaders were inclined to suspect those who claimed to experience the direct working of the Holy Spirit. Church officials became fearful of spiritual excesses and unbridled enthusiasm. They preferred order to what they regarded as the chaos of Montanism. So official Christianity responded to Montanism by developing a priesthood, into which one entered only by the official laying on of hands.

In many ways the church did a heroic job in its

first three centuries. We owe a great debt to the early church for the attention it gave to orthodoxy, stability, and order. The church successfully resisted persecution and, in spite of numerous martyrdoms, continued to grow. On the minus side, however, the church failed to teach about the work of the Holy Spirit within the Christian. One result was that the subject of spiritual gifts was almost completely neglected.

In the age of the church fathers, Augustine represented the typical attitude toward spiritual gifts. When Augustine commented on the gifts of the Holy Spirit in his *Confessions,* he failed to do justice to the biblical texts on this subject. He lacked any consistent or precise discussion of the spiritual gifts listed in the New Testament, and he minimized the place of the Holy Spirit in imparting divine enabling to Christians. Augustine and the other church fathers were at best vague in dealing with the meaning and place of spiritual gifts in the church.

When the Emperor Constantine was converted to Christianity in A.D. 313. he actively began to make Christianity a state religion. Once he had united the church and the state, both institutions changed radically. Whereas the church had once been composed of a persecuted minority, it now found itself in a majority position. The church faced a new set of problems as hundreds of thousands of nominal members hastily joined its ranks. It was suddenly required to develop ways to instruct and guide its new converts. As a result, official Christendom strengthened its concept of the priesthood, giving priests "powers" to absolve penitents and to administer the sacraments, which were regarded as the primary means of grace. People were made completely dependent upon the clergy.

The strong emphasis on the ordained ministry created a chasm between priest and people, resulting in a dependent and passive laity. In time, clericalism became top-heavy, eventuating in a centralized bureaucracy, headed by a pope.

As time passed, spiritual gifts continued to receive little emphasis. The church launched the Crusades, during which time (950-1350) it resorted to wars and cruel persecution to make converts and to regain lost lands. Vital religion slipped even further into the background when the medieval church unleashed the Inquisition. The Inquisition sought to crush heresy and schismatic groups which were seeking religious renewal by emphasizing a direct personal experience of the Holy Spirit, apart from the ministries of the church.

During the period from the Emperor Constantine to the Protestant Reformation (313-1517), the accepted way of expressing spirituality was

13

through monasticism. Other unacceptable expressions of spiritual hunger surfaced through a series of protesting renewal groups, all of which parted ways with the church.

During the Middle Ages one such renewal group blossomed into the sect of the Waldenses. Members of this group denounced the abuses of ecclesiastical power and sought to revive vital religion. They stressed the importance of laymen, they rejected prayers to the saints, and they protested against the heavy emphasis on the Mass. This group embraced some nonbiblical views—not so much because of improper motives, but because they lacked guidance.

From the church's point of view, the Waldenses and other similar sects posed a threat to institutional religion. Therefore, the pope refused to sanction the activities of these groups. In the end, the church either crushed them or forced them into schism. Lacking stability, these groups eventually died out, leaving only monasticism, which continued to rank as the highest expression of devotion to God.

Although monasticism made some important contributions to the Christian church, its orientation was so vertical that it neglected the horizontal aspects of the Christian faith. Because of its cloistered way of life, it had little need to develop any theology of spiritual gifts.

Thomas Aquinas, a monk and a representative theologian of the medieval Roman Catholic Church, drew a parallel between spiritual fruits and spiritual gifts. He defined *charisms* (gifts) as "gratuitous graces," and equated spiritual gifts with inner virtues such as love and hope. Thomas Aquinas' views became the standard for most of Roman Catholicism. Thus, traditional Roman Catholicism failed to develop an adequate theology of spiritual gifts.

During the Protestant Reformation of the sixteenth century, the Lutheran and Reformed theologians seldom mentioned spiritual gifts, if at all. When Luther discussed spiritual gifts he identified them with talents or material blessings. At best, Luther was imprecise in his infrequent discussions of spiritual gifts. For instance, he wrote that the ability to read other languages is a spiritual gift. Luther's teaching on spiritual gifts, taken as a whole, seems as vague as the teaching of Thomas Aquinas.

John Calvin, commenting on the spiritual gifts listed in Romans 12:6-8, wrote, "It does not appear that Paul intended here to mention those miraculous graces by which Christ at first rendered illustrious his gospel; but, on the contrary, we find that he refers only to ordinary gifts, such as were to continue perpetually in the church." Calvin failed to clarify what he meant by "ordinary gifts," but he seems to have been referring to natural, God-given talents.

Calvin stated ambiguously that "all things that pertain to the true knowledge of God, are gifts of the Holy Spirit." He espoused the point of view that the supernatural gifts of the Holy Spirit ceased with the death of the last apostle.

When we come to early Methodism we find an emphasis on the work of the Holy Spirit, but no concern for spiritual gifts. John Wesley wrote, "It does not appear that these extraordinary gifts of the Holy Ghost were common in the Church for more than two or three centuries. We seldom hear of them after that fatal period when the Emperor Constantine called himself a Christian."

Wesley made a distinction between what he called *extraordinary gifts of the Holy Spirit* and *ordinary gifts*. The ordinary gifts he equated with talents and moral virtues, but he remained vague as to the meaning of extraordinary gifts.

Wesley's principal concern was that Christians should concentrate on the "more excellent way"—love. We owe John Wesley a great debt for calling the church's attention to the importance of the Holy Spirit in Christian experience. Perhaps Wesley's passion for holy living and his monumental accomplishments in social reformation did not allow him time to develop a comprehensive theology of spiritual gifts.

Unhappily, the religious controversies that followed the Protestant Reformation hindered the development of a serious theological study of spiritual gifts. Because Christians were preoccupied with doctrinal disputes and religious wars, the gifts of the Holy Spirit never received prominent attention, either in Protestantism or in Roman Catholicism.

Many Protestants of past generations have followed John Calvin in regarding spiritual gifts as temporary manifestations, experienced only in the days of the apostles. The Reformed branch of Protestantism, in particular, has viewed spiritual gifts with suspicion. Reformed theologian Benjamin B. Warfield wrote (Miracles, p. 23), "The extraordinary gifts belonged to the extraordinary office [apostleship] and showed themselves only in connection with its activities."

Whatever contributions earlier theologians have made—and they have been many—a theology of spiritual gifts has not been one of them. The subject is seldom touched on in the writings of most of the Christian leaders of the past.

During the last quarter of the nineteenth century the Holiness Movement (a movement composed largely of Methodists) became interested in the nature of spiritual gifts. At about the turn of the twentieth century the Holiness Movement helped spawn the Pentecostal Movement. The Pentecostal Movement equalled, if not exceeded, the Corinthian church of Paul's day in stressing spiritual gifts. Unfortunately, the Pentecostal Movement tended to emphasize only some of the spiritual gifts listed in the scriptures. (Pentecostal literature of that period discussed the spiritual gifts listed in I Corinthians, but neglected those gifts listed in Romans and Ephesians.) Divine healing and speaking in tongues received special emphasis in this movement. Many pentecostals believed that physical healing was "in the Atonement" and that God always wills physical healing. This movement also insisted that speaking in tongues was a necessary evidence of one's having been "baptized in the Holy Spirit." Speaking in tongues received such stress in pentecostal circles that pentecostalism became known as the "Tongues Movement."

Although pentecostalism helped some people, it tended to fall into the same patterns of subjectivism that had characterized the Montanists of the second century and the Waldenses of the twelfth century. Pentecostalism bred schism; and, using proof texts, pentecostal leaders frequently built their teaching on oral traditions, personal experiences, and a strong desire to see outward supernatural manifestations of the Holy Spirit.

Thus, as a consequence of denominational neglect and pentecostal enthusiasm, the subject of spiritual gifts has suffered much misunderstanding. Sweeping generalizations have been made by those favoring as well as by those opposing an emphasis on spiritual gifts.

Those who have emphasized spiritual gifts have felt misunderstood by those who have not done so. And those who have not made much of a place for spiritual gifts have felt threatened by those who do. In general, misunderstanding has led to criticism, disunity, and loss of objectivity.

Fruitful study regarding any Christian teaching must proceed from a sound biblical base. Of course, we cannot ignore Christian experience, theology, or denominational traditions. But the scriptures must be allowed to speak for themselves and to guide us in our conclusions.

In a new way, Christians are experiencing various spiritual gifts, and are asking perceptive questions about the nature and function of these gifts. One may fairly say that never in the history of the Christian church has there been such a wide-spread interest in the biblical teaching about this vital aspect of the Christian life. For this enthusiasm we can give thanks to the Lord of the church, for out of such interest may come fresh insight and renewed vigor for the people of God.

Chapter II

Biblical Bases for Spiritual Gifts

The Bible does not give us a formal definition of spiritual gifts. It does, however, give us a great deal of insight regarding their nature and function. As in the case of other Christian doctrines, we arrive at a theology of spiritual gifts by putting together the pieces of biblical evidence.

In a general sense, all blessings that come from God may be called "gifts." For example, James wrote, "Every good endowment and every perfect gift is from above, coming down from the Father of lights with whom there is no variation or shadow due to change" (James 1:17). Technically though, a spiritual gift refers to a supernatural enabling of the Holy Spirit which equips a Christian for his work of service and ministry.

Scripture distinguishes between the *gift* of the Holy Spirit and the *gifts* of the Holy Spirit. All Christians receive the *gift* of the Holy Spirit at the time of their conversion to Jesus Christ. In Acts we find Peter saying, "Repent, and be baptized every one of you in the name of Jesus Christ for the forgiveness of your sins; and you shall receive the gift of the Holy Spirit" (Acts 2:38). Believing Christians are born of the Spirit (John 3:6), sealed by the Spirit (Eph. 1:13), and baptized in the Spirit (Eph. 4:5; Acts 11:15-16; I Cor. 6:19). Thus, God bestows the gift of the Holy Spirit upon all Christians. Beyond that, he also imparts spiritual gifts of a wide variety to the Christian community.

When the New Testament speaks of spiritual gifts, it normally uses the word *charismata*. This word is found, for example, in I Corinthians 12:4: "Now there are varieties of gifts [*charismata*] but the same Spirit." The word also appears in Romans 12:6: "Having gifts [*charismata*] that differ according to the grace given to us, let us use them."

Scripture distinguishes between spiritual gifts and spiritual fruit. The fruit of the Spirit (see Gal. 5:22-23) consists of a ninefold cluster of graces—all leading to moral virtues. Spiritual fruit has to do with our relationships and the spiritual quality of our lives. Spiritual gifts, on the other hand, have to do with our calling and our function in ministry. Spiritual fruit relates to what we *are*; spiritual gifts relate to what we *do*.

Spiritual gifts differ from human talents. All

21

persons have natural aptitudes and abilities, but only Christians can receive spiritual gifts. A human talent is, of course, a gift of God. But human talents can function independently of the Holy Spirit. In contrast to a talent, spiritual gifts cannot function apart from the special working of the Holy Spirit. Let's attempt a definition: a spiritual gift is a supernatural ability or capacity given by God to enable the Christian to minister and to serve.

There are a number of New Testament passages relating to the gifts of the Holy Spirit. The major passages are:

> Romans 12:6-8
> I Corinthians 12:4-11
> I Corinthians 12:28
> Ephesians 4:11

(Some additional passages are I Cor. 1:5-7; 12:29-30; 13:8; II Cor. 8:7; I Thess. 5:20; I Tim. 4:14; II Tim. 1:6-7; Heb. 2:4; I Peter 4:10-11.)

A careful study of these passages yields five basic principles regarding spiritual gifts.

1. *God imparts spiritual gifts according to his divine grace; they cannot be earned through human merit.* Christians cannot earn spiritual gifts any more than they can earn the fruit of the Spirit, or for that matter, divine pardon.

The Greek word *charismata* stems from the

word *charis*, which in the New Testament means "grace." God's grace undergirds all the gifts of the Holy Spirit. Paul had this thought in mind when he wrote, "Grace was given to each of us according to the measure of Christ's gift. Therefore it is said, 'When he ascended on high he . . . gave gifts to men'" (Eph. 4:7-8).

Luther's famous dictum, *sola gratia* (by grace alone) applies to every aspect of the Christian life. For this reason, the church is "charismatic" because it participates constantly in the gifts and graces of God. All other societies and organizations may claim some measure of self-creation and autonomy. The church, however, has been created by its Lord. Jesus said, "I will build my church" (Matt. 16:18). The church stands as God's special creation, brought into being by divine grace. Part of Jesus' present ministry is to mature the church and to impart gifts to Christians in order to equip them for effective discipleship.

God has made each Christian a minister in his own right. Obviously, God could build his kingdom by himself—or through the ministry of angels. But he has, in fact, chosen you and me to be his co-laborers (I Cor. 3:9; II Cor. 6:1). God's working in us is not based on our merit. God's call and God's enabling testify to his divine love and continuing grace.

2. *God gives spiritual gifts according to his own discretion; he is not bound by man's wishes.* God always takes the initiative in his dealings with man. Because God cannot be commanded or coerced, we must allow him to remain sovereign Lord in our lives. Scripture encourages Christians to desire spiritual gifts, but it is never appropriate for one to *insist* that God give him a particular gift of the Spirit.

Writing about spiritual gifts, Paul stated that the Holy Spirit "apportions to each one individually as he wills" (I Cor. 12:11). The writer to the Hebrews declared, "God also bore witness by signs and wonders and various miracles and by gifts of the Holy Spirit distributed according to his own will" (Heb. 2:4). These and other verses of scripture teach that it remains God's prerogative to distribute spiritual gifts according to his own wisdom. (See I Cor. 12:18,28; Eph. 4:11; Rom. 12:6.)

Paul compared individual Christians to the members of a body: "For the body does not consist of one member but of many. . . . If the whole body were an eye, where would be the hearing? . . . God arranged the organs in the body, each one of them, as he chose" (I Cor. 12:14-18). The apostle is saying that a body cannot operate properly unless all the members of that body function harmoniously. Maturing

24

Christians are not concerned with who is the most important member of the body. Each person has his unique service to perform. Christ exists as the head of the church, and every Christian is a vital member who fully qualifies as a candidate for the spiritual gifts of God's choosing.

Some Christians yield to feelings of inferiority because they think that their spiritual gifts rank beneath the gifts of others. To such persons Paul said in effect, "There are no unimportant spiritual gifts. Be grateful for the gift God has given you—don't seek to be a copy of someone else. Be an original!" In the church there are no second-class Christians, and there are no super-Christians. While Christians do differ in function, they all stand equal in status. Each believer makes his own contribution to the total church.

Feelings of jealousy and inferiority sap our joy and our genius. Ingratitude for our particular spiritual gift blinds us to the true value of what God has given, and it hinders the creative working of the Holy Spirit in our lives. Dissatisfaction with God's gift underscores spiritual immaturity and our failure to trust his wisdom and grace.

If some Christians feel dissatisfied with their spiritual gifts, others tend to become smug about theirs. These Christians feel superior to those who do not possess the same gifts as they do. In the Corinthian church pride tarnished the attitudes of those who spoke with tongues. They tended to insist that others must also experience that same gift. Paul rebuked such an immature and divisive attitude: "If all were a single organ, where would the body be? . . . The eye cannot say to the hand, 'I have no need of you'" (I Cor. 12:19-21).

The following advice from Paul speaks to all of us: "Do not be conceited or think too highly of yourself; but think your way to a sober estimate based on the measure of faith that God has dealt to each of you" (Rom. 12:3 NEB). Rightly understood, the Christian gospel punctures the balloon of human pride, and creates a community of mutual respect.

There is no more place among Christians for an attitude of superiority than there is for a sense of inferiority. All spiritual gifts come from God, who distributes the *charismata* in the church according to his perfect wisdom.

3. *God wills that every Christian exercise spiritual gifts; these divine enablings are not limited to a few believers.* The gifts of the Holy Spirit are not exclusively for ordained clergymen or for any elite group of Christians—they belong to every member of Christ's body.

Note the following important passages of scripture:

—"To each is given the manifestation of the Spirit for the common good" (I Cor. 12:7).

—"The same Spirit . . . apportions to each one individually as he wills" (I Cor. 12:11).

God intends every Christian believer to manifest spiritual gifts. Receiving spiritual gifts is part of being a Christian.

God distributes different gifts to different Christians: "Now there are varieties of gifts . . . but it is the same God who inspires them all in every one" (I Cor. 12:4-6). All spiritual gifts have their source in God—here is unity. God distributes a plurality of spiritual gifts among the Christian community—here is variety.

Paul illustrated the variety of spiritual gifts this way:

"One man's gift by the Spirit is to speak with wisdom, another's to speak with knowledge. The same Spirit gives to another man faith, to another the ability to heal, to another the power to do great deeds. The same Spirit gives to another man the gift of preaching the Word of God, to another the ability to discriminate in spiritual matters, to another speech in different tongues and to yet another the power to interpret the tongues" (I Cor. 12:8-11 Phillips).

Later in the book we shall look at all the gifts of the Holy Spirit which are specifically mentioned in the New Testament. The gifts just quoted serve to point out the diversity of *charismata* in the church.

Paul emphasized the concept of unity this way: "For just as in a single human body there are many limbs and organs, all with different functions, so all of us, united with Christ, form one body, serving individually as limbs and organs to one another. The gifts we possess differ as they are allotted to us by God's grace, and must be exercised accordingly" (Rom. 12:4-6 NEB). An individual Christian is not likely to possess every gift of the Holy Spirit (I Cor. 12:29-30). Christians are called into community because Christ is our common head and because each Christian needs the ministries of other Christians.

God distributes the gifts of the Holy Spirit according to his wise providence. He offers to each Christian the gifts best suited to his personality. Happy is the Christian who discovers the spiritual gift that God extends to him. Happier still is the congregation in which the gifts of the Holy Spirit are operating in all their diversity and unity.

4. *God provides gifts for the purpose of ministry and service; they are not given in order to draw attention to man or to satisfy his ego.* The bond between gifts and service underscores a consistent biblical principle: God blesses us not so that we may become static or self-serving, but

in order that we may become dynamically active in ministry to others. Jesus taught that if we save our lives we lose them, but if we lose them in service we truly find them.

Paul advised, "Each man is given his gift by the Spirit that he may use it for the common good" (I Cor. 12:7 Phillips). Peter reinforced the importance of gifts leading to ministry when he counseled, "As each has received a gift, employ it for one another, as good stewards of God's varied grace" (I Peter 4:10).

Spiritual gifts exercised apart from service always lead to confusion, immature squabbling, and unhealthy introspection. On the other hand, if we attempt to minister without divine enabling, we will lack the power necessary to accomplish lasting good. Spiritual gifts are not for the purpose of self-gratification or self-glorification. God gives them to us in order that we may serve others.

The presence of a spiritual gift in a Christian does not "prove" his spirituality or his maturity. God gives spiritual gifts (as he gives natural talents) assuming the risk that we might apply them wrongly. Through immaturity, ignorance, or self will, one may misuse his spiritual gift.

Unless we continuously keep our spiritual gifts consecrated to God we risk certain dangers. We may become self-centered and seek to acquire personal glory from our ministry. Or, in our self-seeking, we may attempt to garner power or money from the use of our spiritual gifts. So long as we remember that God gives us spiritual gifts for the purpose of benefiting others, we can avoid these pitfalls.

Thus, a true exercise of spiritual gifts in the church is not marked by flamboyant or spectacular manifestations, but by dedicated service. We can experience New Testament community only through the responsible use of the gifts of the Holy Spirit in mutual edification.

5. *God intends that the ministry of the church be accomplished through spiritual gifts; human talents are not adequate for spiritual ministry.* A tragedy occurs whenever the church seeks to accomplish its ministry while neglecting the gifts of the Holy Spirit. In our own time we can hope that Christians will not resort to unaided human resources to meet the great challenges which face the church. Although organization and human planning remain necessary, in themselves they lack the spiritual dynamic to minister effectively to modern man.

Paul declared, "Weak men we may be, but it is not as such that we fight our battles. The weapons we wield are not merely human, but divinely potent to demolish strongholds" (II Cor. 10:3,4 NEB). Nothing less than the supernatural resources of God will equip the church to meet the opportunities of this generation.

Perhaps the contemporary church should consider the gifts of the Holy Spirit in the light of Jesus' parable in the book of Matthew (25:15-30). In that parable one man was given five talents, another was given two talents, and another was given one talent.

Two of the men made good use of their talents, and one did nothing with what he was given. At the time of reckoning, the lazy and careless servant lost the talent he had. By way of contrast, the faithful servants were rewarded with additional talents. Jesus concluded, "For to every one who has will more be given, and he will have abundance; but from him who has not, even what he has will be taken away" (Matt. 25:29).

Such passages of scripture were certainly not written to discourage the church; they were written to fire the church with courage, hope, and confidence. Jesus offers us his supernatural graces and gifts so that we may be fitted for ministry.

Neglect of spiritual gifts may stem from any of several causes: (1) *Ignorance* of God's provision for equipping the church with spiritual gifts. (2) *Lethargy* concerning God's working in our lives. (3) *Unwillingness* to respond to some aspect of God's call to service and ministry. The neglect of

31

spiritual gifts will stifle personal growth and cripple the ministry of the church.

This is not to say that the church has never used spiritual gifts since New Testament times—such is not the case at all. In some areas, the church experienced what it did not understand. Christians can exercise spiritual gifts without being aware of doing so. Nevertheless, new "light" brings new responsibility. Any failure to take advantage of all of God's known resources will seriously weaken the effectiveness of the church.

When Paul encouraged Timothy to rekindle the gift that God had given him (II Tim. 1:6), he was expressing a basic spiritual law: abilities grow with use, but they atrophy with disuse. Although spiritual gifts are freely given by God, we have a responsible part to play in their development.

God has endowed the church with a plenitude of spiritual gifts so that "Christians might be properly equipped for their service, that the whole body might be built up until the time comes when, in the unity of common faith and common knowledge of the Son of God, we arrive at real maturity—that measure of development which is meant by 'the fullness of Christ'" (Eph. 4:12-13 Phillips).

Paul shepherded churches that faced many of

the same dangers and opportunities that we encounter today. To these early congregations he wrote, "Having gifts . . . let us use them" (Rom. 12:6). His advice pulses with divine inspiration. Through the use of the *charismata* that God offers to you, the Holy Spirit will give you an effective ministry far more significant than you could ever imagine.

Chapter III

How Spiritual Gifts Function

Spiritual gifts function as incarnations of God's power in human life. Sometimes they flow through and heighten our natural abilities, and sometimes they work independently of personal aptitudes. In any case, spiritual gifts complement and blend harmoniously with our humanity.

Some Christians tend to equate spiritual gifts with human abilities. According to this way of thinking, every aptitude that one possesses can qualify as a spiritual gift. Abilities, whether they evidence a spiritual anointing or not, are confused with spiritual gifts. This point of view, though sincerely held by some, falls short of the New Testament teaching regarding the supernatural dimension of spiritual gifts. When we regard every activity as an expression of a spiritual gift we tend to confuse human ability with the working of the Holy Spirit.

At the opposite pole there are equally sincere Christians who tend to overspiritualize the *charismata.* They set aside man's personality and focus exclusively upon the working of the Holy Spirit. Those holding this view tend to see man as overwhelmed by God, and used as his passive instrument. Certainly, this perception of spiritual gifts fails to take into account man's freedom and the importance of human cooperation with God. The biblical concept of spiritual gifts includes both God's power and man's responsible use of that power.

Christianity does not stem from man's endeavors to be good. The dynamic Christian life results from the operation of God's grace in the lives of believing Christians. The Holy Spirit enters into our personalities, not to blot them out but to build them up. He reshapes our humanity as we learn to live in union with Jesus. The unique blend of the divine and the human in the life of Jesus Christ stands as a model for the way God works in our lives. As the *charismata* of God work through our humanity, the Holy Spirit harmonizes our natural selves with his divine gifts.

The following passage of scripture stands out as the best starting point for understanding how spiritual gifts function: "Now there are varieties of gifts, but the same Spirit; and there are varieties of service, but the same Lord; and there are varieties of working, but it is the same God who inspires them all in every one" (I Cor. 12:4-6).

In the passage of scripture just quoted, three important words stand out:

gifts
service (or ministries)
working (or results, or effects)

The inspired writer affirms, first of all, the plurality of gifts in the Christian community. The New Testament clearly indicates that all of the spiritual gifts should operate freely in the church for the purposes of ministry, evangelism, growth, and worship. For these purposes God provides a variety of gifts.

Paul also stated that there are varieties of ministries and varieties of results. By this statement the apostle meant that the various gifts of the Spirit operate in the church through a diversity of ministries. These ministries will produce different results (see page 37).

Spiritual gifts express themselves through various ministries which, in turn, accomplish a variety of results. Let's illustrate this way:

Suppose a person receives the gift of teaching, and he exercises his gift through the ministry of preaching. And suppose another person exercises his gift of teaching through the ministry of writing. A third person may exercise his gift of

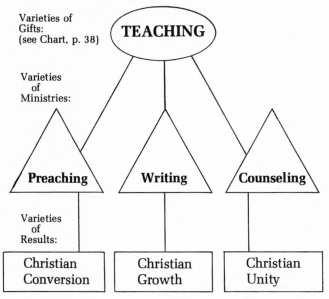

Varieties of Gifts: (see Chart, p. 38)

Varieties of Ministries:

Varieties of Results:

TEACHING

Preaching — Writing — Counseling

Christian Conversion — Christian Growth — Christian Unity

teaching through a ministry of counseling. In each case, the same gift expresses itself through various ministries—preaching, writing, counseling.

These different ministries will likely produce different results: One ministry may lead to Christian conversions; another ministry may aid Christians to grow in grace; and another ministry may heal discord and division. "There are varieties of gifts . . . there are varieties of service . . . there are varieties of working [results]."

When we consider the variety of spiritual gifts

37

A Chart of the New Testament Charismata

Romans 12:6-8	I Corinthians 12:4-11	I Corinthians 12:28	Ephesians 4:11
Prophecy	Prophecy	Prophecy	Prophecy
Teaching		Teaching	Teaching
Serving			
Exhortation			
Giving			
Giving Aid			
Compassion			
	Healing	Healing	
	Working miracles	Working miracles	
	Tongues	Tongues	
	Interpretation of tongues	Interpretation of tongues	
	Wisdom		
	Knowledge		
	Faith		
	Discernment		
		Apostleship	Apostleship
		Helps	
		Administration	
			Evangelism
			Shepherding

and the multiplicity of ministries through which the gifts can operate, we begin to glimpse an enormous potential. As the church allows the gifts of the Holy Spirit to operate in a biblical fashion, there is no limit to the possibilities of God's working.

As we have seen, the spiritual gifts appear in bold relief in four basic scriptural passages. The above chart shows the spiritual gifts that are listed in the New Testament.

A number of the spiritual gifts appear only once in these passages of scripture. Others are mentioned twice; some three times; and one gift appears in all four of these basic lists. Allowing for duplications, the number of spiritual gifts mentioned in these lists totals twenty. The spiritual gifts in the passages of scripture outlined in the chart encompass all of the basic areas of ministry within the church.

Some students of the Bible feel that the spiritual gifts in the above chart are merely suggestive. They believe that there are many other spiritual gifts in addition to the ones just listed. It is quite possible that the twenty gifts outlined above do not constitute an exhaustive list. In this book, however, I am limiting the study to those twenty spiritual gifts found in the four basic biblical passages listed in the preceding chart.

If we move out beyond the *charismata* clearly indicated in the New Testament, we have difficulty knowing where to stop. When we depart from a biblical base we find it almost impossible to avoid speculation. For example, is the ability to usher a spiritual gift? Or the talent for taking care of babies? To be sure, ushers and baby-sitters play an important part in the life of the church, but I do not think that it is technically correct to refer to these ministries as spiritual gifts.

Although spiritual gifts can operate in our lives without our being aware of it, a proper understanding of spiritual gifts serves several good purposes. For one thing, an understanding of spiritual gifts enables you to cooperate with God's working. As you learn to recognize spiritual gifts, you are enabled to receive more intelligently and with greater profit the gift ministries of others. Most importantly, as you grasp the nature and purpose of the *charismata* you can begin to concentrate on what God has called you to do. You will find a greater fulfilment as you cooperate with the stream of God's activity by responding to the work of the Holy Spirit.

The presence of spiritual gifts in one's life is not necessarily a proper measure of Christian maturity or personal holiness. Jesus always insisted that true character is revealed by spiritual fruit (see, Matt. 7:15-20).

Even though spiritual fruit stands out as the most convincing evidence of our Christian faith, spiritual gifts do remain essential for effective ministry. John Wesley once said, "There is no holiness but social holiness." He meant by that statement that the life of Christ within us must express itself contextually in service to others. Like Jesus, Christians are called not to be served, but to serve. The *charismata* are a part of God's equipment for this work.

The precise meaning of some of the spiritual gifts is not obvious to everyone alike. As new generations of Christians arise, they will doubtless understand spiritual gifts better than our generation does. Nevertheless, it is time for the church to give a good deal of thoughtful study to this important subject. Christians must begin to look seriously into these gifts and attempt to understand their basic nature and purpose.

Any division of spiritual gifts into categories runs the risk of being somewhat artificial. Nevertheless, for the sake of study, certain classifications of spiritual gifts may be helpful. In the next three chapters we will divide the twenty spiritual gifts under three headings:

1. The Enabling Gifts
1. The Serving Gifts
3. The Gifts of Tongues and the Interpretation of Tongues

In the final two chapters we will discuss ways to

discover the spiritual gifts that God has for you, and we will look at some suggestions as to how spiritual gifts should be used in the church.

Becoming familiar with the gifts of the Holy Spirit can prove to be one of the most exciting adventures you have ever undertaken. As you study the spiritual gifts you may discover some aspects of the biblical message that will add a new dimension to your Christian experience. It would not be the first time that a fresh study of scripture has worked a quiet miracle.

One of the joys of being alive stems from our capacity to grow. And one of the joys of being in Christ is based on God's making the resources of the Holy Spirit available to his children. As you read further in this study of spiritual gifts, perhaps God will create something new in your life.

Chapter IV

The Enabling Gifts

Now we turn to a detailed examination of the gifts of the Spirit. In this chapter we will examine the *enabling gifts*. These spiritual gifts are found in Ephesians 4:11-12. I am suggesting that we call them the enabling gifts because they are specifically associated with the officers of the church, whose task it is to enable the Christian community to serve and to minister.

There are five enabling gifts listed by Paul: "And his gifts were that some should be apostles, some prophets, some evangelists, some pastors and teachers, to equip [enable] the saints for the work of ministry, for building up the body of Christ" (Eph. 4:11-12). These spiritual gifts stand out as higher gifts because they build up the church and prepare the body of Christ for ministry and service.

Apostleship

The word *apostle* in Paul's day was a common word, understood by his readers to mean "a messenger" or "one who is sent forth." The Latin equivalent for apostle is *missio*, from which we get the word missionary. In some parts of the Eastern Church missionaries are still called apostles. The gift of apostleship refers to a special ability to introduce the gospel to another culture or race and then to nurture the converts in Christian discipleship.

Considerable discussion has developed around the questions of whether there were only twelve original apostles and whether this is yet a gift in the church today. There is a sense in which the original twelve apostles were unique: they formulated Christian doctrine and they laid the foundations for the Christian church. The apostles in the New Testament enjoyed a special relationship with Christ (I Cor. 15:5,7), and they played a role in the formulation of the Christian church that cannot be repeated (Acts 2:42; Eph. 2:20; Rev. 21:14). In one sense the apostolic function ceased at the end of the New Testament era, but in another sense apostolic ministry remains valid in the present church.

In the New Testament the term *apostle* is used for other than the original twelve apostles. In the list of the original twelve apostles (Matt. 10:2-4), Paul is not mentioned. Yet he became an apostle (Rom. 1:1; I Cor. 9:1; II Cor. 12:12). Barnabas, too, served as an apostle, although, like Paul, his

44

name does not appear among the original twelve (Acts 14:14). Additional apostles are mentioned in the New Testament: Andronicus, Junias (Rom. 16:7), James the Lord's brother (Gal. 1:19), Silvanus, and Timothy (I Thess. 1:1; 2:6).

Both Paul and John warn of false apostles (II Cor. 11:13; Rev. 2:2). Such caution would be pointless if the New Testament congregations recognized only twelve apostles. Moreover, in the post–New Testament era, the office of apostle continued in the church.

Thus, the biblical evidence points to the continuing gift of apostleship in the church. This conclusion is supported by most commentators. For example, The International Standard Bible Encyclopedia states, "The apostolate was not a limited circle of officials holding a well-defined position of authority in the church, but a large class of men who discharged one . . . of the functions of the prophetic ministry" (I, pp. 203-4).

We may conclude that the gift of apostleship is given to the church today for its instruction and nurture. Paul seemed to have a continuing apostolic gift in mind when he wrote, "And his gifts were that some should be apostles" (Eph. 4:11).

Apostleship rests not in being one of the twelve or in having descended from the twelve by a special ceremony of the laying on of hands. As an automatic transfer of authority the doctrine of apostolic succession lacks New Testament support. One stands in apostolic succession only if he remains devoted to the apostles' teaching and the fellowship of the Christian community (Acts 2:42). The gift of apostleship cannot be transmitted mechanically by ritualistic means. Its character is personal and spiritual.

The gift of apostleship in the church today equips one to go where Christ directs in order to establish, instruct, and guide local assemblies of believers. This gift differs from that of shepherding (pastoring) in that the pastor performs his ministry in a single congregation. The apostle, by way of contrast, takes the gospel to non-Christian areas, and there he successfully transplants the Christian faith.

In today's world, we can best understand the ministry of an apostle in terms of missionary work. While not all missionaries are apostles, some clearly are. Hudson Taylor stood out as an apostle to China. In recent times E. Stanley Jones was an apostle to India.

Paul seemed to give a place of highest prominence to those with the gift of apostleship (I Cor. 12:28). An apostle is usually gifted with many of the *charismata* because of the heavy demands placed on him and because at first new Christians look to him for all they know about Christianity.

Apostles who assume the difficult task of carrying the gospel across cultural barriers are greatly needed in our time. If the Christian church is to begin to keep pace with the mushrooming world population, it needs the ministry of those especially called and equipped to establish the Christian faith among new groups of people. Happily, God continues to raise up dedicated persons and to anoint them for this task. They deserve our respect and our support.

Prophecy

Biblical references to prophecy indicate that prophecy was rare in the Old Testament, but that it became quite common in the New Testament. The Old Testament contains a number of promises that the day would come when there would be many prophets declaring God's word. A well-known example of these promises may be found in Joel 2:38:

> And it shall come to pass afterward,
> that I will pour out my spirit on all flesh;
> your sons and your daughters shall prophesy.

Peter, in the sermon he preached after the Holy

Spirit's anointing at Pentecost, quoted this verse from Joel and affirmed that it had become a reality in the church (Acts 2:16-18). Among the prophets in the New Testament congregations some were church officers and some were laymen.

The Old Testament prophets were spiritually and socially sensitive. They spoke about the evils of their day, and became involved in correcting them. They stressed both inward righteousness and social righteousness. Old Testament prophets preached relevant messages which helped shape people's consciences. Although the prophets sometimes suffered for their faithfulness, they stood firmly as God's spokesmen, declaring the full counsel of God.

Prophecy means basically to speak God's word with divine anointing. In the scriptures, prophecy is used far more to proclaim than to predict. To be sure, telling of future events sometimes was involved in prophesying. However, the relevant presentation of God's word to the immediate situation dominates the greater share of New Testament prophecy. The gift of prophecy ranks as one of the higher gifts of the Spirit given to the church by the resurrected Lord (Eph. 4:8,11; I Cor. 12:28; 14:19).

In today's church prophecy may be equated largely with inspired speaking in behalf of God, sometimes from clergymen and sometimes from laymen. Prophecy may include a review of the past and a word about the future; but prophecy fundamentally means *light for the present*. Effective prophecy communicates God's word to men in the midst of their current situation.

Not all prophecy comes from God. John the apostle warned, "Many false prophets have gone out into the world" (I John 4:1). Paul also warned against false prophets, insisting that all prophecy be tested. All prophets are subject to error, and the congregation has a responsibility to reject false prophecy and false teaching. Paul insisted that when prophets speak for God, "let the others weigh what is said" (I Cor. 14:29). In I Corinthians 14 Paul gave the following guidelines for evaluating prophecy:

1. Prophecy will edify or build up the congregation.
2. Prophecy will encourage and impart life.
3. Prophecy will console believers and draw them toward God in Christian unity.

The New Testament consistently teaches that Christian prophecy will be orderly, positive in orientation, and edifying to the church.

True prophets are not arrogant. They are willing to have their prophecy examined in the light of the Bible. Biblical prophets did not claim authority for their own opinions; they began with "Thus says the Lord." In our time, the church's primary touchstone for judging the validity of prophecy is the Bible. Prophets who are truly inspired by God will speak words that harmonize with scripture, and they will apply the biblical message positively and redemptively to man's current situation.

Valid prophecy never becomes ecstatic or uncontrollable. In Paul's day some prophets became frenzied or fell into trances. Some, in their dazed state, went so far as falsely to prophesy, "Jesus be cursed!" (I Cor. 12:3). No true prophet loses control of himself and speaks things of which he is unaware. "The spirits of prophets are subject to prophets," insisted Paul, "for God is not a God of confusion but of peace" (I Cor. 14:32-33).

Prophecy remains enormously important in our day because it constitutes one of God's most common ways of bringing a congregation face-to-face with God's truth and of encouraging persons to respond to the living Lord. Paul wrote to the Christians at Corinth, "Earnestly desire the spiritual gifts, especially that you may prophesy" (I Cor. 14:1). Elsewhere he advised, "Do not despise prophesying" (I Thess. 5:20).

Current prophecy will not result in a new revelation—holy scripture remains normative for the church's doctrine. Prophecy will, however, bring new inspiration and illumination as it is spoken under the anointing of the Holy Spirit. Prophecy remains an important avenue through which God presently addresses modern man. Blessed is the congregation that hears and heeds the inspired word of God.

Evangelism

The word *evangelism* stems from a Greek root, meaning "to proclaim good news." Thus, the basic task of evangelism is not to thunder a message of God's wrath and judgment. Rather, evangelism refers to the positive presentation of the message of God's grace and his gospel of healing love.

Certainly, all Christians are called to be Christ's witnesses (Acts 1:8). Each believer has been commissioned by God to be an "epistle" of divine grace seen and read by all others (II Cor. 3:2-3). The words and the actions of every Christian should call attention to God. Nevertheless, the gift of evangelism is given to some Christians to endow them with an unusual capacity to lead others into a saving relationship with Jesus Christ. The gift of evangelism is a special ability that helps one to bring the gospel with remarkable success to the unconverted.

51

In our time, much discussion has centered around the importance of social involvement with the needs of oppressed people. Occasionally the stress on meeting human need has led some to insist that the church should give only a "nonverbal witness." Evangelism has been understood by such persons to mean "Christian presence," without oral proclamation. The rationale behind such thinking is that human needs are too pressing to spend time preaching. Some have gone so far as to suggest that the church has no right to intrude into the private religious beliefs of other persons, insisting that the church's sole task is service.

Such a concept of evangelism, however, fails to harmonize with New Testament teaching. In the scriptures verbal proclamation of the good news of God's love remains basic to Christian evangelism. While we must not divorce the Christian message from active involvement in meeting human need, we must not overlook the mandate of Christ to preach the kingdom of God and to make disciples of all nations (Matt. 28:19-20). At the heart of effective evangelism rests the church's responsibility to proclaim the good news. Pursuing this line of thought, Paul wrote, "How are they to believe in him of whom they have never heard? And how are they to hear without a preacher? . . . faith comes from what is heard, and what is heard comes by the preaching of Christ" (Rom. 10:14,17).

In the book of Acts, Philip stands out as an example of one who displayed the gift of evangelism. This layman was led by God to move from place to place where his gift was needed. Apparently, Philip did not possess the gifts of shepherding and teaching; God used others to establish and to instruct the converts. But God used Philip's gift of evangelism to lead persons to Christ.

Today we need full-time evangelists as well as a host of dedicated laymen with this spiritual gift. Evangelism may take the form of public speaking or one-to-one witnessing. Evangelists deserve the moral and financial support of the church. Only with the operation of the gift of evangelism can the Christian church success-fully win the unconverted masses of our genera-tion to Jesus Christ.

Shepherding

Three words for the pastoral ministry of shepherding are used interchangeably in the New Testament: *episcopos*, which means "over-seer" or "bishop"; *presbuteros*, which means "elder"; and *poimen*, which means "shepherd."

The terms "bishop," "elder," and "shepherd" are synonyms in the New Testament. Shepherd refers to what one does; overseer refers to how one does it; and elder refers to the place the shepherd has in the Christian community.

The office of pastor is not an appointment of men; it is an appointment of God. Therefore, one should have a divine call of God for the task of shepherding a flock. The church ought not to think of the pastoral ministry as a profession. It is a calling. If one's calling from God is valid, it will be recognized by the congregation and by one's fellow shepherds.

The primary task of the shepherd is to feed, to guide, and to minister to a community of Christians. The pastor is called to serve, not to be served. He is called to equip and to enable the body of Christ for its life in the world (I Peter 5:2-3).

The New Testament requires that a pastor be "blameless; . . . not be arrogant or quick-tempered or a drunkard or violent or greedy." He should be "hospitable, a lover of goodness, master of himself, upright, holy, and self-controlled." Pastors also are to hold firm to the sure word, be apt at teaching, and be able to defend the Christian gospel (Titus 1:7-9).

The pastor is responsible for the nurture of those in his care. Warning of false shepherds who teach false doctrines, Paul told the Ephesian elders, "The Holy Spirit has made you overseers, to care for the church of God" (Acts 20:28). Jesus told Peter, "Tend my sheep" (John 21:16). Peter, in turn, urged other shepherds, "Tend the flock of God that is your charge . . . being examples to the flock" (I Peter 5:2-3).

The pastor is not to dictate to the congregation, nor is he to drive his people. God requires him to nurture those in his charge, to lead them, and to provide for them. Jesus' discussion of a shepherd is found in John 10:1-18. In this passage Jesus says that the shepherd sacrifices for his sheep; he goes before them and he protects them.

The gift of shepherding is not limited to clergymen. Laymen, too, may have this spiritual gift. Some laymen who possess the gift of shepherding perform a vital ministry by feeding and guiding others in Christian discipleship. Every active pastor should welcome all the help he can get in shepherding his people in the way of Christ. A true pastor recognizes "under shepherds" who greatly expand the ministry of Christ and significantly enrich the fellowship of the Christian community.

The gift of shepherding takes its place among the highest of God's spiritual gifts to the church. Without this gift, no clergyman should seek to lead a Christian congregation. When this gift is operating in the dedicated pastor, he faithfully leads the congregation in the ways of Christ so that the Christians in his care will mature in Christ under his sanctified labors.

Teaching

Another very important enabling gift is teaching (Eph. 4:11). The gift of teaching equips one to impart truth to others in a relevant way so that the gospel can be understood and applied to life. The teacher in the church can effectively communicate the truths of Christian faith so as to make truth live for others.

The church requires sound teaching if it is to maintain spiritual health. Jesus asked us to love God with our minds as well as our hearts (Matt. 22:37). We must constantly grow in our understanding of truth because faith that rests solely on experience or emotion remains shallow. Teachers are communicators of God's truth, and only by the truth can we really be free.

Among Jesus' final words to his disciples are these: "Go therefore and make disciples of all nations, baptizing them in the name of the Father and of the Son and of the Holy Spirit, teaching them to observe all that I have commanded you" (Matt. 28:19-20). The apostles felt that teaching was so vital that they continued to instruct even though they faced severe persecutions (Acts 4:17-21; 5:40-42). Paul spent an entire year teaching at Antioch (Acts 11:26); he stayed a year and six months teaching at Corinth (Acts 18:11); he remained two years at Ephesus, teaching the people (Acts 19:10). Teaching occupies a large part of the activity and content of the New Testament.

James warned, "Let not many of you become teachers, my brethren, for you know that we who teach shall be judged with greater strictness" (James 3:1). Peter wrote, "There will be false teachers among you, who will secretly bring in destructive heresies, even denying the Master who bought them, bringing upon themselves swift destruction" (II Peter 2:1). False teachers in the church have historically spawned disunity and confusion, creating many of the scandalous divisions in Christ's body. True teachers, on the other hand, bring clarity and unity. Through their ministries we receive help, edification, truth—and life.

The good teacher is both content-oriented and learner-oriented. To emphasize content alone results in an impersonal and sometimes irrelevant presentation. To stress only the learner and relevant methodologies tends to result in a shallow content. The good teacher brings together both content and learner in a creative way.

Good teaching rests on scripture, and it leads others to a personal application of biblical principles in their own lives. The result of good teaching is growth and development in the body of Christian believers.

We have seen that the enabling gifts of the Holy Spirit should not be thought of as belonging exclusively to clergymen. Laymen, too, may manifest these gifts. Few persons, however, will likely possess every enabling gift of the Spirit. God distributes his gifts across the church with perfect wisdom. The gifts of the Spirit studied in this chapter stand out as basic to the ministry of the church because they equip the body of Christ for its larger ministry in the world.

Apostleship meets the need of the church to transplant the Christian message to other lands and other cultures. *Prophecy* is given to inspired speakers and writers so that the Word of God may come in power to Christian believers. *Evangelism* enables the Christian community to reach non-Christians with the good news of Christ's saving love. *Shepherding* makes possible the nurture and guidance of the people of God. *Teaching* provides the body of Christ with understanding so that all believers may grow into maturity.

As the gifts of the Spirit function in the church,

Christians will be properly equipped for their service, "that the whole body might be built up until the time comes when, in the unity of common faith and common knowledge of the Son of God, we arrive at real maturity—that measure of development which is meant by 'the fullness of Christ'" (Eph. 4:12-13 Phillips). As this miracle takes place, the church will begin to fulfill its destiny. In the power of the Spirit it will truly become God's invincible army for the salvation of humanity.

Chapter V

The Serving Gifts

"Whoever would be great among you must be your servant" (Matt. 20:26). With these words Jesus underscores one of the most revolutionary aspects of his teaching: greatness comes not through being served, but through serving. In God's kingdom the standard of achievement is found not in exercising power over others, but in ministering to them.

Jesus dramatically illustrated this teaching by washing his disciples' feet (John 13:12-16). Members of God's kingdom follow the example of their Lord, who "came not to be served, but to serve" (Matt. 20:28). As we have seen, the New Testament regards all Christians as ministers and servants. Each Christian is given spiritual gifts so that he may contribute to the body of Christ in a special ministry.

In this chapter we shall examine the serving gifts which are listed in the New Testament. These gifts, if properly understood and faithfully exercised, will add a new dimension to the Christian church.

The Word of Wisdom

The gift of the word of wisdom has to do with a divine illumination that enables one to apply God's truth to an immediate problem or need. The gift of the word of wisdom differs from the gift of the word of knowledge. The word of knowledge has to do with an inspired insight about a fact, a situation, or a context. The word of wisdom, on the other hand, enables one to apply spiritual truth to a concrete situation in a specially anointed way so that others recognize that truth has been spoken.

To be sure, all Christians are invited to ask for God's wisdom when they need it (James 1:5). The gift of the word of wisdom, however, is a special power given only to some Christians, enabling them to apply spiritual truth to a specific issue in an especially relevant fashion.

In a supreme way, Jesus possessed this gift. When the Pharisees sought to confuse or trick him, Jesus got down to the roots of their questions. He answered them with such wisdom that he penetrated into the hidden implications of their questions (Luke 13:17; 14:6; 20:40).

The gift of wisdom transcends innate human insight or human philosophy. Paul wrote that the wisdom of this world is foolish when compared to God's wisdom (I Cor. 1:20-25). Paul himself

61

possessed the gift of wisdom. His writings and his recorded conversations give evidence of this gift in his life.

Stephen, too, possessed the spiritual gift of wisdom. God enabled him to speak with great insight to his confused persecutors. Luke records, "They could not withstand the wisdom and the Spirit with which he spoke" (Acts 6:10). Stephen's wisdom, however, was not accepted, and his opponents killed him. The Jews' response to Stephen underscores an important principle: even though one speaks God's Word in great power and wisdom, there is no guarantee that others will receive it.

Sometimes the word of wisdom is given in specific situations as a word of divine insight for the moment. At other times, the word of wisdom undergirds an entire presentation of spiritual truth. The gift of the word of wisdom has a wider application than we sometimes think. I believe that anointed speaking and writing will regularly incorporate elements of this spiritual gift. It is through this gift that God enables one to communicate his truth in such a way that it penetrates effectively into the hearts of other people.

The person who exercises this gift may not have any more formal learning or innate genius than others. But he is given the ability to discern a situation and speak the wisdom of God for clarification and encouragement.

Naturally, the presence of this gift in the church does not imply that study and scholarship should be neglected. God normally combines the inspiration of the Holy Spirit with dedicated talent and work. The combination of consecrated human activity and the divine anointing of the Holy Spirit results in effective Christian activity. When the gift of the word of wisdom is properly manifested it accords with scripture, and it edifies others because for them it has the ring of truth.

The Word of Knowledge

Whereas the gift of the word of wisdom involves the application of spiritual truth, the gift of the word of knowledge enables one to understand or grasp the truth about a situation or a spiritual principle. In short, this spiritual gift imparts the ability to perceive a fact as God sees it. Sometimes wisdom and knowledge are spiritual gifts given to the same person, and the two often function in a complementary manner.

The scriptures contain numerous instances showing the gift of knowledge in operation. Jesus exercised this gift during his conversation with the woman at the well. He told her facts about her personal life that he had no way of knowing, except by divine insight (John 4:16-26). Peter demonstrated this gift when he made his great confession to Jesus: "You are the Christ, the Son of the living God." Jesus affirmed Peter's confession by saying, "Blessed are you, Simon Bar-Jona! For flesh and blood has not revealed this to you, but my Father who is in heaven" (Matt. 16:16-17).

From time to time, present-day Christians also receive this spiritual gift. Quite a few persons have told me that while counseling another person, they received a divine word of knowledge about the other person—an insight that they had no way of knowing except by the direct working of the Holy Spirit. When one senses that God has given him a fact that will help him to minister, he has probably received a word of knowledge for the occasion.

This spiritual gift should not be confused with magic or spiritual clairvoyance. Such powers are often claimed by non-Christian spiritualists. The true gift of the word of knowledge comes from God, never from spiritualist mediums or from psychic powers.

God never gives any spiritual gift so that we can take advantage of another person or embarrass him. Any insight into the personal needs of others should be carefully used in a private context, never as a display or a show. Flamboyant public uses of this gift have no place in Christian ministry.

Christians who receive this gift need to use it gratefully, always with humility and a desire to minister. God gives the word of knowledge to Christians today so that they may be equipped to bring God's truth into focus in our contemporary world. This spiritual gift is given to the end that we may more effectively mediate the grace of Christ to human need.

Faith

To a degree, all Christians have faith. Paul wrote, "For by grace you have been saved through faith" (Eph. 2:8). Without faith, in fact, we cannot properly relate to God (Heb. 11:6). While all Christians possess the *grace* of faith, not all Christians possess the *gift* of faith.

The gift of faith is given to some Christians as a special ability to see the adequacy of God and to tap it for particular situations. This spiritual gift produces an extraordinary confidence in God—a confidence which draws upon his divine resources. The Christian who possesses this gift of the Spirit has a supernatural conviction that God will reveal his power in response to the prayer of faith.

Faith does not, of course, arise out of the cauldron of our subjective imaginations. We cannot muster up faith by merely working at it. Faith comes by responding to God's prior working in our lives. As Paul put it, "Faith comes from what is heard, and what is heard comes by the preaching of Christ" (Rom. 10:17). Paul is saying that for faith to be engendered, God must first inspire our confidence in him. Then on "hearing" God speak, we believe and accept God's promise. The common way that God communicates the gift of faith is by his speaking to us through the Bible; and the common way we exercise faith is through prayer.

Through faith in God all Christians can avail themselves of his provision for their lives, but the gift of faith goes beyond a mere general affirmation of God's promises. The gift of faith takes hold of biblical principles, and under the inspiration of the Holy Spirit applies them to the current situation. The gift of faith enables one to believe God for mighty results.

Faith is not limited to getting things from God. It extends to believing God even in the dark hours. For example, when on the cross, Jesus did not exercise faith so that God would release him from his ordeal. Rather, he believed God to work something significant through his suffering and dying. Profound faith trusts God to redeem the past, the present, and the future—even when darkness temporarily surrounds.

The person who has the gift of faith should not chide others for their lack of faith. After all, not every Christian possesses this gift. Rather than berate others for their lack of faith, the Christian with this gift should lift the burdens of others and appropriate God's adequacy for them.

Christians with the gift of faith often love to spend long hours in prayer. (Great preachers usually have those with the gift of faith praying faithfully for them, believing God for important results.) The person with this gift may not always receive a great deal of attention, but his exercise of faith remains essential for the well-being of the entire Christian community.

Gifts of Healing

The gift of healing enables one to function as an instrument of God's healing grace in the lives of others. Certainly, this spiritual gift does not equip one to heal in every instance. The Bible teaches that, as a result of man's fall, suffering and death are a part of our human and earthly condition. These enemies will completely pass away only when God establishes a new heaven and a new earth (Rev. 21:4). We need not feel that we have failed if prayer does not always result in physical healing. Frequently God works differently than we expect him to work.

God heals in five ways:

1. God heals instantly and directly.
2. God heals gradually through the processes of nature.
3. God heals through medical science.
4. God gives grace to suffer redemptively by healing our attitudes.
5. God heals in the resurrection.

In the scriptures we find numerous examples of miraculous healing (see, Matt. 10:1; Acts 3:7; 5:16; 9:34; 14:10; 16:18; 28:8). Other biblical examples can be found where God does not grant physical healing (see II Cor. 12:7-10).

Well-meaning but ill-informed Christians have insisted that God wills to heal all persons physically, and if one is not healed, he lacks faith or clings to unconfessed sin in his life. Such assertions have created enormous problems for Christians who remain unhealed physically, even though they harbor no known sin and even though they place their faith in God for healing.

Although Paul prayed for physical healing, he was not directly healed as he wished. In Paul's case God gave him the promise, "My grace is enough for you." Reflecting on his disappointment, Paul wrote, "I have cheerfully made up my mind to be proud of my weaknesses, because they mean a deeper experience of the power of Christ" (II Cor. 12:9 Phillips).

Certainly, Paul's sickness did not stem from sin or lack of faith. Nor did Lazarus', nor Timothy's, nor that of Epaphroditus. Jesus, in fact, observed that some infirmities work for the glory of God (John 9:3). In our finite understanding we are not always able to know or to explain the will of God with respect to physical healing. After all, 100 percent of mankind eventually does die.

In scripture we are encouraged to place faith in Christ's *ability* to heal, not his *willingness* to heal. Jesus never asked, "Do you believe that I am willing to heal you?" He did ask, however, "Do you believe that I am able to heal?" One does not lack faith because he is uncertain about God's will concerning physical healing. It does show a lack of faith, though, if we doubt God's *power* to heal.

Mark has an interesting passage illustrating what I mean. The father of a sick boy came to Jesus, explaining that Jesus' disciples were unable to heal him. Then the father of the sick boy said, "If you can do anything, have pity on us and help us." Jesus did not like that prayer at all!

Immediately, Jesus replied, "If you can! All things are possible to him who believes."

The father of the sick boy exclaimed, "I believe; help my unbelief!" Immediately after this affirmation Jesus healed the sick boy (Mark 9:15-29).

The point of this discussion is that we presume upon God when we insist on telling him when and how to heal. Although none of us knows fully God's *will* with respect to physical healing, we can affirm that God has the *power* to heal. The person with the gift of healing exercises this gift properly when he places his faith in God's power, then trusts the results to him.

God often works through human vessels, combining natural and supernatural ministries. I believe that we have a clue for understanding God's normal way of bringing about physical healing in the book of James: "Is any among you sick? Let him call for the elders of the church, and let them pray over him, anointing him with oil in the name of the Lord" (James 5:14).

The word James uses for "anoint" is *aleipho*, which means "to oil the skin by rubbing," a medical practice common in the East. James does not use the word *chrio*, which means "a ritualistic or symbolic anointing." Before the days of miracle drugs such as penicillin, rubbing with oil was one of the most widely accepted medical remedies known to man. I believe that the rubbing with oil to which James referred was a commonly accepted medical practice used on sick persons.

James was saying, in effect, "Use prayer and use the best medical know-how available—both methods of healing come from God. But do all 'in the name of the Lord,' for God is the source of all healing." My conclusion is that we should use both medical and spiritual means in the ministry of healing. Man can perform surgery or administer wonder drugs, and man can pray and give spiritual aid—but it is always God who heals.

Perhaps God sometimes withholds healing because of man's frequent tendency to become preoccupied with miracles or human agents. On numerous occasions Jesus asked the people to tell no one of his healings. Jesus made those requests probably because of man's tendency to become absorbed in miracles and lose sight of the One who produces the miracles. Jesus wants us to trust him for what he *is* rather than for what he *does*.

The apostles had to resist the tendency of some to place them on a pedestal because of their healing gifts. Gifts of healing should lead us to focus our attention on God who heals, never on the agents he chooses to use.

The gifts of healing certainly allow for the use

of medical doctors. At times, of course, God transcends all human endeavors, and supernaturally ministers his healing grace to human hurts. The gifts of healing extend to the body, to the emotions, and most important of all, to the deep recesses of the human spirit.

Workings of Miracles

There are numerous examples of the gift of workings of miracles in the scriptures. Like the gifts of healing, this spiritual gift also appears in the plural form. The plural wording suggests that each miracle is a special gift, given as needs and occasions arise.

Neither Jesus nor the disciples ever exercised this gift as a spectacle, merely for the purpose of drawing attention to themselves. In the New Testament miracles were sometimes used to draw people to a commitment to God (Acts 13:11-12); and sometimes they were used simply to meet human need (Matt. 14:14-21).

Jesus said to his disciples, "he who believes in me will also do the works that I do; and greater works than these will he do" (John 14:12). Soon after Pentecost this gift became operative in the church. Luke records, "Signs and wonders are performed through the name of thy holy servant

Jesus" (Acts 4:30). He later recorded, "God did extraordinary miracles by the hands of Paul" (Acts 19:11; see also I Cor. 2:4).

In all candor, we must confess that instances of water being turned into wine, persons walking on the water, or physical resurrections from the dead are not common occurrences in our time. Doubtless God is able to work such miracles among us; but it is safe to say that we do not regularly experience the sort of miracles which occurred in the book of Acts.

Why?

For one thing, our faith has been clouded by our tendency to offer scientific explanations for all things. We have overreacted against an earlier generation of people who saw God's hand directly intervening in virtually every matter. Even the movement of the tree tops and the occurrence of thunderstorms were seen as acts of God. We have moved beyond such a simplistic understanding of nature. Modern man tends to account for almost every aspect of his experiences in terms of scientific explanations. Our naturalistic view of reality has produced a secular mentality. This anti-supernatural bias doubtless hinders God's miraculous working in our time.

Christians are convinced that they serve a supernatural God, one who works miraculously in the lives of men. In one sense miracles are the daily experience of Christians; but in another sense Christians walk by faith, not by sight. Fundamentally, Christians do not rely upon what God does, but who he is.

Although God continues to work miracles in our time, miracles are not required to validate the Christian message. The church itself has become God's sign to our age. *Changed lives* remain the greatest possible demonstration of God's miraculous working in our world.

My feeling is that when external miracles occur today, they will most frequently happen in the context of an unevangelized mission field. In completely non-Christian areas, God may, from time to time, suspend what we understand to be the laws of nature in order to certify his message or his messenger. But as Christians mature, they become more interested in moral and spiritual miracles than in physical and outward ones.

Certainly, Jesus placed a higher priority on spiritual regeneration than he did on works of power. On one occasion, for example, Jesus said, "Which is easier, to say, 'Your sins are forgiven you,' or to say, 'Rise and walk'? But that you may know that the Son of man has authority on earth to forgive sins"—he said to the man who was paralyzed—"I say to you, rise, take up your bed and go home" (Luke 5:23-24). Jesus frequently refused to do miracles because he wanted persons to base their faith in him, not in what he did.

Some Christians point to the singular passage in Mark 16:16-18 as a basis for Christians to cast out demons, to speak with tongues, to handle deadly snakes, to drink poison without ill effects, and to receive answers to all prayers for physical healing. We must remember, however, that the closing verses of Mark's Gospel (verses 9-20) do not appear in the oldest and best manuscripts. In the Greek manuscripts that are extant, Mark's Gospel stops with verse 8 of chapter 16. The passage in question reads remarkably unlike the rest of Mark. Therefore, because of these two reasons, their non-inclusion in the ancient manuscripts and their striking dissimilarity to the rest of Mark, all reputable commentators agree that no doctrine should ever be derived from these uncertain verses.

Nowhere in the New Testament are we urged to seek signs. In Paul's passages on Christian maturity, miracles are never mentioned. Jesus spoke these arresting words: "This generation is an evil generation; it seeks a sign" (Luke 11:29). It is immature to insist on demonstrations of a physical nature, when we have an even greater miracle available to us—spiritual regeneration! The greatest supernatural manifestation of all is that human life can be reshaped by the power of the risen Lord.

Most certainly, God can and does work miracles. However, Christians should not spend a great amount of time fretting if physical miracles do not occur in their churches or in their lives. Few converts were ever won in biblical times by miracles: Moses' miracles only alienated the pharaoh. Even the Hebrews soon came to take for granted the miracle of the daily manna which God gave to them during their wilderness journey. Soon after Jesus fed the five thousand it became apparent that the followers were only interested in free handouts (John 6:26-27, 66). Lazarus' resurrection from the dead did not impress the religious leaders; rather it resulted in a plot to crucify Jesus (John 11:53).

In a classic passage, Jesus gave his assessment of miracles: "If they do not hear Moses and the prophets, neither will they be convinced if some one should rise from the dead" (Luke 16:31). Christians who become preoccupied with signs and miracles should remember that we are called to walk by faith, even when there *seems* to be no visible evidence of God's working.

God normally acts in and through natural means. In a sense, any event becomes miraculous when God works in it to accomplish his purposes. God's perfect timing in natural events is as much a miracle as his superceding the laws of nature. Truly, God is at work in our lives in all places and at all times, both in divine providence and in spiritual transformation. That working in itself should qualify as the highest sort of supernatural activity.

Discernment

The gift of discernment is the ability to distinguish between spirits, whether they are divine, human, or demonic. The gift of distinguishing between spirits is not necessarily the ability to tell whether someone else is a Christian. This spiritual gift does equip one to discern a Christian spirit or a non-Christian spirit in order to prevent confusion and false teaching from infiltrating the church.

Satan often appears as a counterfeit agent of truth. Emphasizing this thought, Paul wrote the following statement: "Even Satan disguises himself as an angel of light. So it is not strange if his servants also disguise themselves as servants of righteousness" (II Cor. 11:14-15).

In our day thousands of astrologers are plying their trade, many newspapers carry horoscope columns, and some people in the church are tempted to dabble in occult practices, in seances, and in "communing" with other spirits. Even more subtle than these practices are the claims made by religious leaders who say they are prophets, but whose messages deceive and lead into error.

In such times as these, we are reminded of Jesus' solemn statement, "False prophets will arise and show great signs and wonders, so as to lead astray, if possible, even the elect" (Matt. 24:24). Supernatural activity does not necessarily originate with God. Satan, too, can perform great feats through those who are under his influence (Luke 4:6; Acts 26:18; II Cor. 4:3-4; II Thess. 2:9). Certainly, the gift of discernment is needed in today's church.

Paul, speaking of the increasing stress to come in the church, wrote, "Now the Spirit expressly says in the later times some will depart from the faith by giving heed to deceitful spirits and doctrines of demons" (I Tim. 4:1). He also emphasized that Christians "are not contending against flesh and blood, but against principalities, against the powers, against the world rulers of this present darkness, against the spiritual hosts of wickedness in the heavenly places" (Eph. 6:12). Without a gift of discernment in the church, the people of God are open to all sorts of odd teachings and false doctrines.

While the existence of Satan is a reality,

unfortunately some well-meaning but poorly informed teachers have given Satan far more credit than he deserves. These persons insist that most Christians have areas of their lives that are "possessed by demons." I personally take strong exception to such unwarranted statements— scripture does not support them.

Jesus stated, "No servant can serve two masters; for either he will hate the one and love the other, or he will be devoted to the one and despise the other. You cannot serve God and mammon" (Luke 16:13). How unthinkable that a child of God who is walking in obedience to Christ could at the same time also host demons.

Scripture does not support the notion that Satan is the cause of all our problems. Even when a Christian falls into a sin, this by no means suggests that he is possessed by a demon. We must make a clear distinction between being tempted or oppressed by Satan, and being *possessed* by Satan.

Nor is mental illness necessarily caused by demonic possession. Christians are subject to mental illness just as they are subject to physical disabilities. It is very harmful to say to a depressed Christian, "The reason you are depressed is because you are possessed with demons." While Satan sometimes does cause mental problems, by no means is this always the case. Satan cannot possess the personality of one who is trusting in Christ. Even in the lives of non-Christians, demon possession, though possible, is rare. The enemy can enter our lives only if we permit him to do so.

I personally have never encountered a demon-possessed person. I do know of some cases, however, that have been related to me by mature Christian ministers and missionaries. When exorcism was used, the persons were delivered. In one case the person afterward became a Christian; in another case the person did not. The casting out of demons does not make one a Christian any more than mending a broken leg will make one travel in the right direction or prevent his breaking the leg again.

In the cases of exorcism just mentioned, the Christian workers did not attempt to cast out demons alone, they prayed with the aid of several mature Christians. In each case the workers stated their hope that they would never again find it necessary to go through such an experience. My friends' attitudes toward exorcism contrast sharply with those who blithely scamper about looking for demons to cast out. A great deal of harm has been done to sincere Christians who have been told that the problems in their lives stem from their being possessed with demons.

Perhaps the greatest immediate enemy of the church is the false teacher. Religious teachers may unknowingly sow seeds of error and false doctrine. Often we are impressed by their enthusiasm or their sincerity; but we fail to test the content of their teaching by scripture. The church needs Christians with the ability to discern spirits, whether or not those spirits come from God.

Sometimes we begin to feel uneasy when we hear a teaching or read a book. We may not know exactly what is wrong, but we feel an immediate and instinctive rejection of the spirit of what we hear or read. The spirit of the teaching seems to have an evil or untrue ring. This feeling may well be the gift of discernment at work within us.

All Christians have a responsibility to heed John's advice: "Beloved, do not believe every spirit, but test the spirits to see whether they are of God; for many false prophets have gone out into the world" (I John 4:1). Some Christians, for whom we thank God, have been given a special gift of discernment. They have a divine enabling from God that equips them in a unique way to distinguish between the spirit of truth and the spirit of error.

The gift of spiritual discernment not only enables one to discern evil, but also to discern *good*. Jesus perceived good in Nathanael (John

81

1:47); Barnabas saw good in John called Mark (Acts 15:36-39). If we place too much emphasis upon demons, we place too little emphasis on seeing good in other Christians and in situations and events. Since God is actively at work in the world, we should remain sensitive to his working in the lives of others and in our daily affairs.

We need the ability to discern good in Christian traditions other than our own. Congregations and denominations from time to time become ingrown, and they stand in need of fresh truth. Sometimes we seem slow to recognize and appropriate new truths if they come from another branch of the church. The operation of the spirit of discernment will give approval to teaching and preaching that brings fresh truth from God. In the church we need to concentrate on the pluses more than the minuses.

Without the gift of discernment operating in the church, the Christian community would be totally vulnerable. So long as falsehood and evil insinuate themselves into the life of the church, this gift provides an invaluable ministry among those who name Jesus as Lord.

Helps and Serving

Although the gifts of helps and serving are separate gifts, they are closely related. The gift of

82

helps (I Cor. 12:28) stems from a Greek word *antilapseis*, which means a "support" or a "help." The gift of serving (Rom. 12:7) comes from the Greek word for deacon, which means "one who serves."

The gift of helps leads to person-centered ministries, while the gift of serving equips one for task-oriented ministries. No hard and fast dividing line should be drawn between these two spiritual gifts, although each gift has its own sphere of operation.

Neither of these gifts may seem on the surface to be very glamorous, but each of them provides an indispensable contribution to the life of the church. These gifts do not normally function in a public way like the gifts of prophecy or teaching. Nevertheless, without their operation the church could not function. Perhaps Paul was referring to these gifts when he observed, "If all were a single organ, where would the body be? As it is, there are many parts, yet one body. . . . the parts of the body which seem to be weaker are indispensable" (I Cor. 12:19-20, 22).

Generally speaking, persons who possess the gift of helps are equipped by God to relieve temporal and spiritual burdens. The gift of helps enables one to see the needs of others and to respond willingly to the opportunity to minister.

The gift of serving usually leads one to supply

material and temporal services to the Christian community. In the book of Acts prominent attention is given to those who serve: "The twelve summoned the body of the disciples and said, 'It is not right that we should give up preaching the word of God to serve tables. Therefore, brethren, pick out from among you seven men of good repute, full of the Spirit and of wisdom, whom we may appoint to this duty . . .' And what they said pleased the whole multitude [church] and they chose [seven laymen]" (Acts 6:2-5). In that account, the Christian community chose Spirit-filled laymen with the gifts of wisdom and serving to minister to temporal needs. In the early church Christians were assigned tasks which were suited to their talents and their gifts.

The person who possesses the gift of serving will familiarize himself with community needs and community resources. His gift equips him to meet the physical and material needs of others in a gracious and selfless manner. Persons with this gift remain alert to opportunities to minister in a wide variety of ways.

The gifts of helps and serving lead to the kinds of ministries to others that relieve them of burdens and enable them better to serve Christ. In the New Testament these gifts operated through such widely differing ministries as delivering a package (II Tim. 4:13) and praying (II Cor. 1:11). Many laypersons in the church possess the gifts of helps and serving. Numerous open doors of opportunity beckon to those endowed with these important *charismata*.

Administration and Giving Aid

Two closely related spiritual gifts are administration (I Cor. 12:28) and giving aid (Rom. 12:8). The term for the gift of administration comes from a Greek word meaning a "pilot" or a "steersman." The gift of administration equips one to lead in matters of church organization and government. The person possessing this gift is enabled to direct and organize a larger group of Christians so that each one is released to perform his ministry without the hindrance of disorganization.

The gift of giving aid is translated diffferently in various versions of the Bible:

"he that ruleth" (KJV)
"the man who wields authority" (Phillips)
"he who gives aid and superintends" (Amplified New Testament)
"he who gives aid" (RSV)

The root meaning of the Greek term for this gift is "he who stands before." The best translation of the term is possibly, "he who takes leadership in giving aid." The possession of this spiritual gift enables one to see needs and then to assume leadership in the Christian community in giving aid to meet those needs.

Leadership in the church stands in contrast to a secular understanding of leadership. In secular leadership we think in terms of a boss, or one who rules over others. By way of contrast, the spiritual gift of administration equips one to serve. This spiritual gift does not cause one to order others around carelessly; administration is a serving gift.

Denominational officials, school administrators, pastors, and laymen with church offices would do well to study Paul's qualifications for leaders in the church (I Tim. 3:1-13). The biblical requirements for leaders stress the *quality of one's life* above all other factors. Because time is needed for the cultivation of an exemplary life, the church does not normally elevate newly-converted Christians to administrative offices.

Fortunate indeed is the church where the gifts of administration are in proper operation. In our time, our dislike for authoritarianism and our concern for democracy can cause us to overreact against legitimate authority. We sometimes seek to function without proper leadership. A smoothly functioning body cannot operate without guidance. It is the duty of the members of the congregation to recognize the gift of administration, gratefully accept those with leadership gifts, and follow their Spirit-filled administration. The writer of the letter to the Hebrews advised, "Obey your leaders and submit to them" (Heb. 13:17).

Naturally, the person who has the gift of administration must exercise his gift in love. One should never behave dogmatically or unkindly in leading others. Administrators should serve in humility and wisdom, always seeking to coordinate the gifts and ministries of others for the common good. The administrator must be willing to spend long hours in hard work, giving attention to detail, with little concern for receiving credit for his service. This gift enables one to serve others in a leadership capacity so that the varied ministries in the church will function smoothly for the glory of Christ and the good of the church.

Exhortation

The word translated *exhortation* stems from the same root from which we get the words "advocate" and "comforter." It is, in fact, the same word that Jesus used to describe the Holy Spirit *(Paraclete)*. Perhaps the best contemporary translation of this word is "encouragement."

The gift of exhortation equips one for a ministry of calling forth the best that is in others. Exhortation does not mean dwelling on others' weaknesses or shortcomings; and certainly exhortation does not mean berating others or shaming them. The function of this spiritual gift is to lift up, encourage, strengthen, and admonish another to become his best self in Christ. The gift of exhortation enables one to help others to develop ways of growing spiritually.

Persons often discover this gift in themselves when others gravitate to them for encouragement, consolation, and guidance. This gift is usually exercised in private conversation, although it may sometimes be exercised publicly.

An outstanding illustration of this gift may be seen by looking at Barnabas, who was called the son of Encouragement (Acts 4:36). This Christian worker helped John called Mark to succeed after he had failed in his work. Barnabas' encouragement of Paul helped the great apostle perhaps more that we will ever know.

Naturally, God provides us with our ultimate source of strength, but he often uses others to help us. "You'll do better next time," and "Let's look at ways to improve," are words of exhortation that have helped change lives for the better in countless instances.

One possessing the gift of exhortation does not regard himself as superior to others. The possession of this spiritual gift enables one to identify with another and feel deeply with him. This gift never leads the exhorter to dominate; it enables him to respect the dignity and integrity of those with whom he works.

The gift of exhortation is practical in its working. Those expressing this gift seek to find effective and workable steps of action in order to lead others to greater maturity. The gift of exhortation renders one capable of viewing such serious problems as failure and persecution as stepping stones to Christian growth.

This neglected spiritual gift is finding a new place in the life of the church. Christians who possess the gift of exhortation are able to combine scriptural principles and human experiences in creative and helpful ways. We can be grateful for Christians who manifest the gift of exhortation. They move among us in their quiet way, sowing the seeds of hope and cultivating a harvest of maturing Christians.

Giving

The gift of giving is, like all the other spiritual gifts, a special enabling from God, given to some

Christians for helping others. Of course, all Christians are called to be generous (I Cor. 16:2; Rom. 12:13; Matt. 10:8). But the gift of giving empowers one in a special way to understand the material needs of others, and then to meet those needs generously. The gift of giving is a God-given capacity to give materially for God's work so that others are helped in their lives and ministries.

Paul gave direction concerning the gift of giving: "he who contributes, in liberality" (Rom. 12:8). The word translated *liberality* can mean "unpretentiously," "freely," or "with delight." The pharisees gave to others in order to gain reward and respect, but the gift of giving empowers one to give for the sheer love of helping others. Often the one possessing this spiritual gift will discover that his giving has harmonized exactly with the prayers of those he has helped.

The gift of giving operates on a highly spiritual plane. Those possessing the gift of giving contribute with discrimination. They do not give unwisely or because they are motivated by pity, fear, or pride. As a part of their stewardship they investigate needs, and they seek God's guidance in their giving.

Sometimes those with this gift tend to appear frugal, because in meeting the needs of others they do not spend more than is necessary on themselves. They often give anonymously, and their ministry frequently passes unnoticed by others. Liberality, however, brings its own inner joys and rewards. Those with the gift of giving find that, as they give to the needs of others, they themselves become happy and fulfilled. They also discover that God continues to supply them with the resources to make further giving possible.

Through personal experience, Christians with this spiritual gift have proved the truth of Jesus' words, "give, and it will be given to you; good measure, pressed down, shaken together, running over, will be put into your lap. For the measure you give will be the measure you get back" (Luke 6:38). The gift of giving produces a love burden that expresses itself in the sharing of one's resources freely in the service of God and neighbor.

Compassion

Jesus placed compassion high on his list of desirable qualities that should characterize all Christians: "Blessed are the merciful, for they shall obtain mercy" (Matt. 5:7). Paul, too, stressed the importance of compassion: "Bear one another's burdens, and so fulfil the law of Christ'' (Gal. 6:2).

The gift of compassion transcends both natural human sympathy and normal Christian caring. This gift stems from a special working of God's love deep within one's self. To a profound degree this *charisma* enables one to feel mercy for those in need. This *charisma* results in practical acts of compassion. Christians possessing the gift of compassion both care and share.

Paul expressly stated that mercy is to be exercised with cheerfulness (Rom. 12:8). Doing charitable deeds in the spirit of genuine caring is the divine formula for ministering to those in distress. The performance of an act of mercy with resentment seriously pollutes much of the good that is done.

Even though secular welfare work relieves some hardship, the church of Jesus Christ remains the primary agency for mending broken human spirits and ministering to the physical needs of others. The church must combine spiritual ministry with temporal ministry, and temporal ministry with spiritual ministry. Properly understood, the two cannot be separated.

The gift of compassion equips one to sense in others such emotions as joy, happiness, pain, and despair. Persons with this gift provide a supportive ministry. They remove spiritual turmoil from others and bring them healing comfort. The gift of compassion usually moves one to minister to mental and spiritual needs, although this concern often manifests itself in tangible acts of mercy. The helping of others in distress assumes a more important place than "showing them the truth." Persons who possess the gift of compassion tend to see good motives in others, even when their actions are less than acceptable.

Christians with the gift of compassion often feel led into a special ministry of intercessory prayer. These sensitive souls pray for others and they minister by displaying an attitude of love and mercy. In their unique way, they constitute an indispensable part of the body of Christ. Their work may lack earthly acclaim, but as they minister to the deep hurts of others in the Spirit of Jesus, their work never goes unnoticed above.

In this chapter we have looked at the serving gifts. Some of these gifts lead to public-speaking ministries and some lead to service ministries. Working together in harmony, they contribute to the proper functioning of the body of Christ.

Peter's advice regarding spiritual gifts should be recalled at this point: "Whatever gift each of you may have received, use it in service to one another, like good stewards dispensing the grace of God in its varied forms. Are you a speaker? Speak as if you uttered oracles of God. Do you give service? Give it as in the strength which God supplies. In all things so act that the glory may be God's" (I Peter 4:10-11 NEB).

The church will begin to function more fully as God intended when spiritual gifts resume their rightful place within the life of the congregation. Spiritual gifts are given by God for a twofold purpose—to build up the body of Christ and to equip it for ministry (Eph. 4:12). When the spiritual gifts function properly in the church we have a much better prospect of fulfilling the prayer that Jesus taught his disciples—"Thy kingdom come, Thy will be done, On earth as it is in heaven" (Matt. 6:10).

Chapter VI

The Gifts of Tongues and Interpretation of Tongues

Few spiritual gifts have been discussed so extensively or misunderstood so radically as the gifts of tongues and interpretation of tongues. These gifts have sometimes led to exaggerated emphases, and in some cases they have even divided congregations. Some Christians who speak in tongues have frowned on Christians who do not, and some Christians who do not speak in tongues have disapproved of those who do.

In my book *Fresh Wind of the Spirit* (Abingdon Press, 1975) I described two improper attitudes toward spiritual gifts that are flourishing in the church. These states of mind are *charisphobia* and *charismania*. These two attitudes apply especially to the gift of tongues. Some Christians fear speaking in tongues and oppose any form of this activity. Other Christians elevate speaking in tongues to a place of undue prominence, regarding the gift of tongues as the sign of one's having the Holy Spirit.

In the book of Acts there are several accounts

of persons being filled with the Holy Spirit. In some instances they spoke in tongues and in some instances nothing is said about speaking in tongues. In the Corinthian church all believers were baptized in the Holy Spirit (I Cor. 12:13), but all did not speak in tongues (I Cor. 12:30). Nowhere in the New Testament are Christians urged to expect to speak in tongues as the evidence of having received the Holy Spirit.

Although speaking in tongues is not a necessary sign of the presence of the Holy Spirit, we have no biblical basis for rejecting this gift. In spite of the fact that the exercise of tongues remains controversial, it is a biblical *charisma*. The purpose of this chapter is to seek to put this spiritual gift in perspective and to offer some suggestions for its proper use.

I believe that there are four kinds of speaking in tongues which may be found today:

1. Speaking in a language unknown to the speaker, but known to those who speak that language.
2. Speaking in a language known only in heaven, and unknown on earth unless God gives a gift of interpretation.
3. Speaking under demonic influence.
4. Speaking in nonrational ecstatic verbiage that is a psychological and human response to a religious emotion.

My opinion is this: some speaking in tongues is of God and it is valid; some speaking in tongues is not of God and it is not valid.

In Acts 2:1-11 we find an instance of speaking in known languages. When God sent the Holy Spirit in his fullness at Pentecost, the disciples spoke in at least twelve recognized dialects. Luke reported that bystanders "each one heard them speaking in his own language" (Acts 2:6).

Over the years, I have discussed with friends our experiences of hearing speaking in tongues. Some have reported instances during prayer meetings when someone suddenly spoke in a strange tongue. No one in the group understood what was being said, with the exception of a single international student. In the few instances when persons gave such an account, they reported that the international student heard the prayer in tongues in his own language. Furthermore, the student was deeply moved. While I have not personally witnessed such an incident, I have no reason to doubt what was reported to me by these first-hand witnesses. Perhaps you, too, have heard such accounts.

Cases like the one just mentioned appear to be rare; but apparently they have taken place. This kind of speaking in tongues seems to be almost an exact duplication of the kind of speaking in tongues that occurred in Acts 2. Under special and unusual circumstances when a visitor cannot readily grasp the language being spoken, I see no reason to doubt that God might enable one to pray in a language that could be understood by another knowing that language.

A second kind of speaking in tongues takes place when one prays in a language that seems to have a rational content, but which is unknown to the speaker or to any one present. Apparently this type of tongues parallels what happened in the Corinthian church (I Cor. 14).

This second variety of tongues requires an interpretation if it is to be exercised publicly. Most Christian leaders agree that this variety of praying in tongues should be called *devotional tongues* and it is best reserved for use in one's private times of prayer.

Discussing this type of praying in tongues, Paul wrote, "He who speaks in a tongue edifies himself, but he who prophesies edifies the church. . . . in church I would rather speak five words with my mind, in order to instruct others, than ten thousand words in a tongue. . . . if there is no one to interpret, let each one of them keep silence in church and speak to himself and to God" (I Cor. 14:4, 19, 28).

This much seems certain: a *truly valid* gift of tongues means praying in a language. The language may be known to men, as was the case with the type of tongues found in Acts (2:8); or the language may be unknown to men, and known only in heaven (I Cor. 13:1). Any authentic gift of tongues will not result in babbling or ecstatic rambling; it will issue in a language, either known or unknown.

A third variety of speaking in tongues is prompted by demonic influences. Witch doctors and pagan priests often speak in tongues during wild and immoral religious rituals, often under the influence of drugs. Moreover, instances of speaking in tongues occur regularly among spiritualist mediums and witch doctors.

In Paul's day, temple prostitutes of the pagan religions spoke in tongues as a ritual preparation for their consecrated tasks. In their frenzies, they regularly broke forth in ecstatic utterances. Some scholars suggest that this is the reason Paul advised the Corinthian women not to speak in church. Elsewhere, Paul did not forbid women to talk during the meetings of Christian assemblies. In fact he made provision for them to pray and to prophesy (I Cor. 11:5). Paul's statement that "the women should keep silence in the churches" (I Cor. 14:34), is found in his only discussion of tongues in the New Testament. Perhaps Paul did not want any one to mistake the ecstatic utterances of the Christian women for those of the pagan prostitutes.

Thus, some ecstatic utterances are plainly demonic. Obviously such demonic speaking in tongues does not flow from the Holy Spirit.

A fourth variety of speaking in tongues may be described as psychological. This kind of ecstatic speaking is rooted neither in a divine manifestation of the Holy Spirit nor a demonic manifestation of evil influences. The sort of speaking in tongues I refer to here is a purely human response to religious emotion. Tongues of this sort are closely akin to the shouting which occurred in some of the nineteenth-century camp meetings. We find a similar emotional response to excitement at football games when the favorite team scores a touchdown.

Such verbal responses appear most often when they are encouraged, when they are expected, and when they give one status in a group. It is well known that most groups (religious and non-religious) develop a certain ethos, or expected behavior pattern. Group pressure fosters the operation of the psychological laws of suggestion and imitation. In some of the nineteenth-century revivals one was expected to shout if he were truly converted to Christ. Many were converted under this teaching, and they did shout! The laws of suggestion and imitation work powerfully in combination with group expectation and approval.

Let's look at other examples. It seems quite probable that when the Quakers "quaked" with religious emotion and when the Shakers "shook" with religious emotion, these religious phenomena stemmed from a human response to a sense of the divine presence.

Or take another example: In John Wesley's early ministry some people began to faint with religious emotion during his meetings. This phenomenon was called being "slain in the Spirit." Wesley took a dim view of this activity, and he forbade it. After Wesley began to discourage such demonstrations, the instances of fainting soon disappeared. Wesley could have encouraged fainting by asserting, "If you really are converted to Christ you'll surely faint as a sign that the Holy Spirit has come into your life." Or, he might have appointed ushers to be prepared to catch those who might be "slain in the Spirit." Doubtless, such a climate of expectancy would have caused thousands to begin to faint and thousands of others to seek the "blessing of fainting." Such was not the case: Wesley discouraged the practice, and it stopped. Wesley was far more interested in moral transformation than in physical demonstrations.

In some circles today speaking in tongues is both encouraged and expected as proof of one's having been filled with the Holy Spirit. When a climate of this sort is nurtured one can readily see how such preparation could produce a rash of interest in speaking in tongues. Teaching that includes speaking in tongues as an expected part of the Christian life results in a psychological conditioning which makes speaking in tongues an approved and accepted response to God.

This kind of speaking in tongues is neither of God nor of Satan—it is purely a human reaction to religious emotion. Perhaps a fair percentage of the current interest in speaking in tongues is of this psychological variety.

Having said all this, we must still make a place for the gift of tongues to function among Christians. It is a biblical gift, and there is no reason to be fearful of it, if it is truly given by the Holy Spirit. Most certainly, we are wrong to dismiss what we have not experienced as being of the devil.

Although Paul made a place for the public use of tongues, he carefully regulated its use by giving detailed restrictions. The public use of tongues has given rise to a great number of difficulties and problems. It remains essential, therefore, that we understand the circumstances in which the public use of tongues might be appropriate.

In Paul's lengthy discussion of tongues (I Cor. 14) we find that this gift has three purposes: (1)

prayer (verse 14), (2) praise (verse 15), and (3) thanksgiving (verse 16). All of these uses denote prayer that is directed toward God. Thus, as we have noted, this gift normally should be practiced in private. In public, Christians are advised by Paul to speak in the language of the people (I Cor. 14:19).

The phrase "message in tongues" does not appear in the Bible. So far as I can determine from the scriptures, God does not give *messages* in tongues; he gives utterances in tongues.

A message conveys the idea of God sending a word to the community through a speaker. Neither Luke nor Paul gives a single instance of God giving direct messages to people through the gift of tongues. In the New Testament, tongues serve as a means of worship as a person prays to God in an unknown language. "For one who speaks in a tongue speaks not to men but to God" (I Cor. 14:2).

On the day of Pentecost those who heard the disciples speaking in tongues heard them speaking of "the mighty works of God" (Acts 2:11). And at Caesarea during the so-called Gentile Pentecost, those speaking in tongues were heard "extolling God" (Acts 10:46). In both cases the speaking in tongues consisted of praise and thanksgiving directed upward to God, not outward to man.

103

God does not send messages to the congregation through the gift of speaking in tongues. He gives messages through such gifts as prophecy and teaching. Therefore, tongues are to be directed to God, not man. Prayer, praise, and thanksgiving (biblical uses for this gift) are addressed upward to God. Any interpretation which purports to be a message from God to man is, from the biblical standpoint, highly suspect. Any interpretation of a tongue, if it is to accord with scripture, should interpret the utterance in tongues in terms of a prayer or words of praise or thanksgiving to God.

The gift of interpretation of tongues is the ability to translate or interpret an utterance in tongues. The obvious purpose of interpretation is to turn the congregation's attention away from the one speaking in tongues and focus the worship of the congregation toward God. When tongues are used, the worship of God becomes possible only if the congregation understands the meaning of what has been uttered.

Paul required an interpretation of tongues for every public use of this gift. "If any speak in a tongue," he insisted, "let there be only two or at most three, and each in turn; and let one interpret. But if there is no one to interpret, let each of them keep silence in the church and speak to himself and to God" (I Cor. 14:27-28).

Paul also insisted that there must be order in the public use of tongues. Obviously, the use of tongues ought not to interrupt the speaker in charge of the service, and the one who speaks in tongues should always remain under his authority. "God is not a God of confusion but of peace. . . . all things should be done decently and in order" (I Cor. 14:33, 40).

Most of us tend to think that God should work in others' lives as he does in our own. For that reason, those who receive the gift of prophecy tend to look upon prophesying as the most important activity in the church. One who has the gift of helps tends to think that the major task in the church should be serving others.

In a like manner, Christians who have spoken in tongues sometimes say, "You just don't know what you're missing until you, too, speak in tongues." These Christians often tend to make other Christians feel uneasy or as if they have not experienced the fullness of the Holy Spirit. It is never proper to try to force a spiritual gift on another. If God desires to give someone a spiritual gift, the Holy Spirit is quite capable of creating a desire and leading that person into that gift.

Christians should not make anything foundational to the Christian faith except Jesus Christ himself. The New Testament vigorously discourages divisions among Christians (I Cor. 1:10-13). We simply do not need a teaching movement, a spiritual discernment movement, a helps movement, or a tongues movement. The only movement that Jesus founded was the church!

Paul plainly stated, "Do not forbid speaking in tongues" (I Cor. 14:39). We must, therefore, affirm tongues as a valid gift. But the gift of tongues is not a *required* gift, any more than the other gifts are required. Consequently, we dishonor God if we insist that all Christians speak in tongues. To make such a requirement of every believer would compare with a teacher insisting that all persons manifest the gift of teaching in order to prove that they were filled with the Holy Spirit. Paul likened the various gifts in the church to the various members of the body. What sort of church would we have if all members had the same gift? "If all were a single organ, where would the body be" (I Cor. 12:19)?

Sometimes it is said that the gifts of tongues provides an ecumenical common denominator that will unite Christians. Perhaps those who have made such statements have not thought through very carefully the implications of such a notion. How could speaking in tongues, if practiced by spiritualists, Hindus, Mormons, and animists, serve as a rallying point for Christian unity?

Our unity does not rest on any ecstatic experience; it is based on the person of Jesus Christ. As we draw nearer to Jesus, we will draw nearer to one another.

The well-known dictum with respect to speaking in tongues—seek not, forbid not—seems to sum up the New Testament teaching on this subject. Some Christians have found a new closeness to God as a result of their experience of speaking in tongues. Many other fruitful and creative Christians have never spoken in tongues. I believe it is inappropriate to try to assess who are better Christians, using as a criterion whether or not one speaks in tongues. Paul advised against our comparing ourselves among ourselves (II Cor. 10:12).

The Scriptures call us to keep our attention focused on Jesus, the living Lord. As we abide in him and he in us, we manifest the gifts and graces which flow from his presence within. Because we are free on the inside we can look forward expectantly to God's working in us as well as in our brothers and sisters in Christ. As we participate in the unfolding drama of God's redemptive love, we can affirm in word and deed the praise of him who has brought us into life and given us a place among those who are sanctified by his grace.

Chapter VII

Discovering Your Gifts

No one ever grasps the full scope of the Christian life at the very outset of his commitment to Jesus Christ. Along with other aspects of Christian experience, spiritual gifts are usually discovered as one matures in Christian discipleship. As it takes time to discover and to learn to use our natural talents, it also takes time for Christians to identify and begin to use the spiritual gifts that God has for them.

The Christian life expands constantly as God continues to work within us. Sometimes spiritual gifts lie undiscovered and unused for years. We need, therefore, continually to remain in a receptive attitude so that we may grow. I have been suggesting in this book that an important part of your Christian growth is receiving and using spiritual gifts.

In this chapter we shall look at six guidelines that will aid you in discovering the spiritual gifts that God has for you.

1. *Open yourself to God as a channel for his*

use. Christians seeking to discover their spiritual gifts should begin by affirming that the Holy Spirit dwells within them. Paul wrote to the Christians at Corinth, "Do you not know that your body is a temple of the Holy Spirit within you, which you have from God?" (I Cor. 6:19). Spiritual gifts cannot be separated from their source; all the spiritual gifts exist in the Holy Spirit. The gifts of the Spirit are not like a cassette which God shoves into you. They result from the operation of the Holy Spirit who dwells within every Christian. Spiritual gifts must always be seen in the light of the inner working of the Holy Spirit.

The Christian's proper attitude to the Spirit's presence is a willing surrender to his gracious working. We begin to discover our spiritual gifts as we consecrate ourselves daily to Christ for his using. The spirit of the following prayer is appropriate: Jesus, I affirm that you are Lord. I'm your willing instrument to be used as you see fit. Show me what gifts you have for me, and teach me to be responsive.

Are you unsure of your spiritual gifts? James advised, "If any of you lacks wisdom, let him ask God, who gives to all men generously and without reproaching, and it will be given him" (James 1:5). As you pray about your spiritual gifts, take time to listen to God. Be available.

109

Study the spiritual gifts listed in the New Testament, and then ask God to show you what gifts are yours. You'll be surprised at how readily he responds to your seeking.

2. *Examine your aspirations for Christian service and ministry.* Serving others is, after all, the whole purpose of spiritual gifts. Peter counseled his readers, "As each has received a gift, employ it for one another, as good stewards of God's varied grace" (I Peter 4:10). Maturing Christians have learned that their greatest satisfaction is not in being served, but in serving. So look at what ministry you are drawn toward. In the light of our discussion of spiritual gifts in earlier chapters, which of the spiritual gifts hold a special attraction for you?

Remember that God's normal way of working is to bring excitement into your life, not boredom. An important theme of scripture is that doing God's will satisfies a basic human hunger (John 15:11). Jesus said, for example, "My food is to do the will of him who sent me, and to accomplish his work" (John 4:34). The Holy Spirit generates a desire within us to do God's will. Maturing Christians grow beyond shallow concepts of discipleship that equate unhappiness with serving God.

One important way in which God reveals his will to us is by giving us inner desires. Paul

110

captured this concept in these words:"For God is at work in you, both to will and to work for his good pleasure" (Phil. 2:13). The psalmist expressed this same thought by writing, "Take delight in the LORD, and he will give you the desires of your heart" (Ps. 37:4). God's way is the way of fulfillment—and it is the way of joy! So take seriously your aspirations and spiritual desires. Those inner impulses most likely stem from the promptings of the Holy Spirit.

3. *Identify the needs that you believe to be most crucial in the life of the church.* Another aspect of discovering the spiritual gifts God has for us is the examination of our concerns. God often guides us by creating within us a sense of burden for a task that needs accomplishing or for some need that remains unmet.

The person who is troubled about false doctrines in the church may have the calling to teach. One who is burdened when others are hurting emotionally or physically may have the gift of compassion.

I recently asked a young woman this question: "What do you think is the greatest need in your church?"

She answered, "It concerns me a lot that persons' needs are not met. I think we ought to serve others more than we do."

From observing this young woman and by

talking to others about her, it became obvious to me that she had the gift of helps.

A true shepherd becomes concerned when his people are misled, confused, or divided. Someone with the gift of administration is especially troubled by disorganization and mismanagement. The Christian who has the gift of giving becomes uneasy when resources are unavailable to carry on God's work.

Check out your concerns. God is probably speaking to you and helping you discover your spiritual gifts through the needs you see in the church. As you see opportunities to minister, God will often burden you to get involved personally. If God is leading you to act, he will provide you with the necessary *charismata* for the task.

4. *Evaluate the results of your efforts to serve and to minister.* Gifts, like talents, grow as we use them. A clear indication that God has given you a particular spiritual gift is growth in effectiveness as you exercise that gift.

Questions to ask yourself are:
—Am I developing more competence in this area?
—Do opportunities open up for me to exercise this gift?
—Are my efforts producing good results in the lives of others?

Naturally, not everyone will accept your ministry. (Remember, even Jesus' ministry was rejected by some.) But if you are properly using your spiritual gift, you'll find yourself growing in confidence, in ability, and in effectiveness.

A very good sign that God has given you a spiritual gift is that others within the church are helped by your ministry. False modesty about what God is doing in your life may hinder your spiritual growth. So take an honest look at what God is doing through you. The results of your Christian ministry will serve as a good indication of the gifts God is giving you.

5. *Follow the guidance of the Holy Spirit as he leads you into obedience to Christ.* Jesus said, "He who has my commandments and keeps them, he it is who loves me; and he who loves me will be loved by my Father, and I will love him and manifest myself to him" (John 14:21). Elsewhere, Jesus emphasized the importance of obedience in his parable of the talents: "you have been faithful over a little, I will set you over much" (Matt. 25:23).

Obedience to Christ remains crucial to experiencing the fullness of his life. Of course, we should never assume that our obedience will gain us merit; the Christian life rests solidly on grace, not law. Obedience to Christ, however, does open the door for him to lead us into

113

abundant life. Obedience is the root which produces the fruit of a creative life.

God's primary will for each one of us is the sanctification of all aspects of our lives. Paul, inspired by the Holy Spirit, wrote these words: "For this is the will of God, your sanctification . . . May the God of peace himself sanctify you wholly; and may your spirit and soul and body be kept sound and blameless at the coming of our Lord Jesus Christ" (I Thess. 4:3; 5:23). Basically, God's will for us relates more to the quality of our being than it does with the specifics of our doing. Naturally, God does have a personal, customized plan for each one of us; but he also has a general will for all Christians. His will is that the totality of our existence comes under the redeeming lordship of Jesus Christ.

Sometimes we become overly concerned about the spiritual gifts that God wants us to manifest, while overlooking Christ's basic call to obedient discipleship. Obedience to the light we have will lead us into light we do not yet possess. A sure way to know God more clearly is to follow him more nearly. Obedience to present light will lead us into even greater light in the future.

6. Remain alert to the responses of other Christians. The New Testament discussions of spiritual gifts always occur within the context of the body of Christ, the church. Christ is the head

of the church; and Christians make up the various members of his body, each functioning in a needed way. Working in harmony, the members of the body edify one another and they bring glory to Christ who is the head.

Growing Christians realize that God calls them into fellowship with other members of Christ's church. Since no Christian will manifest every spiritual gift, we all need one another (I Cor. 12:27-31). The individual Christian never exists in isolation; he constitutes but a part of the whole body.

We need constantly to maintain a harmonious relationship with other Christians because others often see our spiritual gifts before we do. The affirmation and support of Christian friends will prove of great help to us in discovering and manifesting our own spiritual gifts. One of the most helpful services we can perform for a fellow Christian is to affirm gifts and graces which we see in him.

If other Christians are not helped by your ministry and if they do not affirm your gift, reevaluate what you are seeking to do. But if the Christian community consistently recognizes and receives your ministry, you may be sure God is working in you through a spiritual gift.

Remember this basic principle: God is more interested in us than we are in him. With this

115

basic principle in mind, be available. If you are open to God, in his own time he will lead you into an understanding of your gifts.

You may want to go back over this chapter, applying each point prayerfully to your life. As in all other aspects of our Christian lives, the following promise of Christ remains valid: "Ask, and it will be given you; seek, and you will find; knock, and it will be opened to you. . . . If you then, who are evil, know how to give good gifts to your children, how much more will your Father who is in heaven give good things to those who ask him!" (Matt. 7:7-11).

Do you want to discover your spiritual gifts? God stands ready to give you wisdom and insight. Why not begin to talk to God about this area of your Christian life? If you have time to pray, God has time to listen.

Chapter VIII

Spiritual Gifts and the Church

In this final chapter we will look at how the gifts of the Holy Spirit function in the church. Because the New Testament discusses spiritual gifts in the context of community, we ought never to think of the gifts of the Holy Spirit as operating independently of the supporting body of Christian believers. Although we are converted to Christ individually, our Christian conversion always relates us intimately to every other person who is also Christ's disciple.

Outside the regulative setting of the Christian community, we become vulnerable to imbalance, division, and heresy. Within the fellowship of the institutional church we have historic continuity with the past, we become heir to an enormous treasury of sound doctrine, and we have the advantage of recognized presence in our world.

We must admit that all persons within the church are not following Christ as they should. Nevertheless, local congregations of Christian believers remain God's vehicles of divine grace. Jesus' promise continues with us: "I will build my church, and the powers of death shall not prevail against it" (Matt. 16:18). The ancient church leaders were not entirely wrong when they spoke of God as our Father and the church as our mother. Being members of the church, we need to learn how spiritual gifts work in the context of its fellowship.

Several principles seem clear.

1. *Spiritual gifts should flow naturally out of our union with Jesus.* The gifts of the Holy Spirit have their source in God, not man. God freely gives the *charismata* to us as tools for ministry. Since they flow from God, we do not need to work them up or to act unnaturally in using them.

The Holy Spirit always works in harmony with you, never against your natural temperament. To be sure, God heightens, transforms, and anoints human personality, but he always works in cooperation with your basic nature.

We do not have to be forced into a spiritual gift; the spiritual gifts stem from the inner presence of the living Lord. One never has to whip up a spiritual gift in himself or in others. If it is of God it will flourish without human gimmicks. When God imparts his spiritual gifts to us, he will give them without strained effort on our part.

The Holy Spirit heightens each person's unique individuality because Jesus works in ways that never violate our humanity. As a seed grows into a mature plant, the Christian becomes an authentic expression of the creative grace of God.

Our Christian lives should be characterized by a genuine naturalness. God never stifles or erases our personalities. God's humanizing grace sets us at liberty to express an inherent freedom that flows in a spontaneous manner. As we live in union with Jesus, his gifts will emanate unpretentiously out of our inner selves.

2. *Spiritual gifts should edify others and help them to grow as Christ's disciples.* The Holy Spirit always works toward positive ends, never negative ones. In like manner, spiritual gifts should build up, encourage, and help those to whom we minister.

Spiritual gifts can be misused so as to embarrass or discourage another person. Whenever we flaunt spiritual gifts in an abrasive or rude manner, we are tragically misusing them. The true test of one's proper use of spiritual gifts can be summed up in the following question: "Do I use my gift in a creative and positive way so that others are lifted up and helped by my ministry?" Remember, the Holy Spirit acts graciously and we should do so as well.

Christians need not tell others that they are using spiritual gifts. They should simply use them in an unpretentious way. We need not be concerned about drawing attention to ourselves. Humility should shape our attitude towards our spiritual gifts because they originate in Christ, not in us. The main purpose of spiritual gifts is to minister to others and to point them to God. Christ never imparts spiritual gifts for the purpose of exalting individual persons or movements. Our goal, like Christ's, is not to be ministered to, but to minister.

Properly understood and wisely used, spiritual gifts can aid the development of a community of maturing Christians. The Holy Spirit helps us minister to each other so that we experience mutual growth. When this sort of spiritual health exists in the church, every member of Christ's body receives benefit and the Lord is glorified in the midst of his people.

3. *Spiritual gifts should draw Christians together in unity.* The biblical imagery of the working of spiritual gifts compares with the functioning of the human body. Each member of the body operates in harmony with all the other members of the body. The hand complements the foot; the arm complements the shoulder; the ear complements the eye. No member of the body works independently. The proper function of our body requires the unity and the cooperation of the individual parts.

Serious problems develop if we gather around

the personality of any human leader. The personality cults of secular man should have no place in the church. If we allow ourselves to become polarized around men, we become fragmented. When we orient ourselves around Christ we move toward unity.

Christian unity remains one of the most powerful assets of the church. Spiritual gifts, rightly understood, will aid in unifying Christian believers, not dividing them. As the gifts of the Spirit are rightly used, they will lead us to a greater appreciation of one another and a more profound allegiance to our common Lord.

Sometimes spiritual renewal movements have led to schism within the Christian community. Such division has not come from God; it has come from man. The rediscovery of spiritual gifts in our generation holds promise of new freedom and a new power for the church, but it also introduces the possibility of a new fracture within Christ's body.

Unity in Christ remains the responsibility of all of us. Each Christian should learn to accept as brother or sister all others who are truly in Christ, even if their gifts and theologies differ. For our common good, all Christians need one another. Consensus on a detailed understanding of spiritual gifts is not as essential as our commitment to love, unity, and service.

The institutional church must remain open to fresh breezes of the Holy Spirit and the edifying excitement of renewed Christians. At the same time, renewed Christians must realize that, although the institutional church is sometimes slow to develop new forms, it does provide a needed stability and wisdom. Unity is always a two-way street, and spiritual gifts rightly understood and correctly used will bring us together in common ministry.

4. *Spiritual gifts should receive a balanced emphasis in the church.* Too much or too little emphasis on any aspect of Christian experience leads to imbalance, if not heresy. Spiritual gifts certainly are no exception to this rule.

If we give too much attention to spiritual gifts we run the risk of neglecting Jesus Christ who is the source of our gifts. Moreover, if we cultivate an unbalanced preoccupation with spiritual gifts, we put in jeopardy the cultivation of spiritual fruit.

On the other hand, if we give too little attention to spiritual gifts we neglect an important aspect of the Christian life. As we have seen, the church cannot function as God intends if Christians rely entirely on their human talents. Only through the *charismata* can Christ's disciples receive the divine enabling they need for their ministry.

So, let us not make too much or too little of spiritual gifts. To become a fanatic about spiritual gifts catapults us out into the open sea of confusion; to ignore God's offer of spiritual gifts leads us into the dry dock of ineffective striving.

5. *Spiritual gifts should function from an inner motive of love.* Paul positioned his great chapter on love in the context of spiritual gifts. That very placement contains an important lesson: spiritual gifts are only effective when used in love. An integral part of Paul's teaching on spiritual gifts is that without love spiritual gifts are useless. Love alone gives value to the ministry of the *charismata.*

Without *love* spiritual gifts cater to human pride, and they become perverted. Without *gifts* love lacks the proper tools with which to function. When love and gifts combine, each gives meaning to the other.

Paul insisted that such gifts as tongues, prophecy, knowledge, faith, and giving are no proof of one's Christian character (I Cor. 13:1-3). Unless love becomes the actuating principle behind the use of spiritual gifts, one is but a "noisy gong or a clanging cymbal." Only love gives true value to the gifts of the spirit.

The extraordinary description of love found in I Corinthians 13:4-7 provides the best definition of love in all literature. Those who desire spiritual gifts should study these verses. When love flows through the *charismata*, each believer becomes an agent of grace and blessing to those to whom he ministers. Earnestly desire spiritual gifts, but make love your primary goal (I Cor. 14:1).

Every human being hungers to discover his own uniqueness and to find his special calling in the world. We can rise to our full privilege only as we experience the unhindered working of the Holy Spirit in our lives. God offers the Spirit's *charismata* to us in order that we may function as channels of his liberating grace. The power so evident in the book of Acts remains as fully available to us today as it was to the New Testament church.

Christians have become members of the household of God, joined together in his Spirit and indwelt by his continuing presence. God has provided the gifts and graces of the Holy Spirit to equip his people for their work of ministry to the end that they shall manifest the unity of faith in joy, in holiness, and in power. Doing so, we shall ultimately mature into the perfection of a new humanity which expresses the fullness of the living Lord.

Index